Virtuous Friendship

MISSIONAL WISDOM LIBRARY
RESOURCES FOR CHRISTIAN COMMUNITY

The Missional Wisdom Foundation experiments with and teaches about alternative forms of Christian community. The definition of what constitutes a Christian community is shifting as many seek spiritual growth outside of the traditional confines of church. Christians are experimenting with forming communities around gardens, recreational activities, coworking spaces, and hundreds of other focal points, connecting with their neighbors while being aware of the presence of God in their midst. The Missional Wisdom Library series includes resources that address these kinds of communities and their cultural, theological, and organizational implications.

Series Editor: Larry Duggins

Recent titles

> *The Julian Way: A Theology of Fullness for All of God's People*
> by Justin Hancock

> *Deconstructed Do-Gooder: A Memoir about Learning Mercy the Hard Way*
> by Britney Winn Lee

Forthcoming titles

> *Abide: A Guide to Living in Intentional Community,*
> by Elaine A. Heath

> *Come with Me: Daily Living with a New Monstic Rule of Life,*
> by Wendy J. Miller

> *Coming Back to Life: A Journey of Earth and Spirit,*
> by Susan MacKenzie

Virtuous Friendship

The New Testament, Greco-Roman Friendship
Language, and Contemporary Community

Douglas A. Hume

CASCADE *Books* · Eugene, Oregon

VIRTUOUS FRIENDSHIP
The New Testament, Greco-Roman Friendship Language, and Contemporary Community

Missional Wisdom Library: Resources for Christian Community

Cascade Books
An Imprint of Wipf and Stock Publishers
199 W. 8th Ave., Suite 3
Eugene, OR 97401

www.wipfandstock.com

PAPERBACK ISBN: 978-1-5326-1232-9
HARDCOVER ISBN: 978-1-5326-1234-3
EBOOK ISBN: 978-1-5326-1233-6

Cataloguing-in-Publication data:

Names: Hume, Douglas A., author.

Title: Virtuous friendship : the New Testament, Greco-Roman friendship language, and contemporary community / by Douglas A. Hume.

Description: Eugene, OR: Cascade Books, 2019 | Series: Missional Wisdom Library: Resources for Christian Community | Includes bibliographical references and index.

Identifiers: ISBN 978-1-5326-1232-9 (paperback) | ISBN 978-1-5326-1234-3 (hardcover) | ISBN 978-1-5326-1233-6 (ebook)

Subjects: LCSH: Bible. New Testament—Criticism, interpretation, etc. | Friendship—Biblical teaching. | Friendship—Rome. | Friendship—Greece. | Friendship—Religious aspects—Christianity.

Classification: BS2545.F75 H8 2019 (print) | BS2545.F75 (ebook)

Manufactured in the U.S.A.   JULY 12, 2019

Significant portions of Chapter 5, "Learning to be Friends of God: Narrative Deficiency, Moralistic Therapeutic Deism, and North American Teens (Acts 2:41–47; 4:32–35)" were published as Chapter 13 " 'You Will Fill Me with Joy in Your Countenance': Engaging the North American Ecclesial Context with a Narrative Ethical Reading of Acts 2:41–47 and 4:32–35" in *Ecclesia and Ethics: Moral Formation and the Church,* edited by E. Allen Jones III, John Frederick, John Anthony Dunne, Eric Legewellen, and Janghoon Park; published by T. & T. Clark, an imprint of Bloomsbury Publishing, 2016. Republished by permission.

Contents

Preface and Acknowledgments

In the very beginning of Aelred's second book on *Spiritual Friendship*, we find the abbot turning from the business of his worldly concerns to catch a few moments with his student, Walter, who has been waiting impatiently for him. Noticing his student frowning, rubbing his forehead, and even running his fingers through his hair as he waits, Aelred apologizes for being so busy. "We have to accommodate ourselves also to the ways of men from whom we either expect favors or fear injuries. Now that they have finally departed, I find this seclusion all the more pleasant."[1] In writing this book over a period of several years, there have been many days when I could relate to Aelred's excuses and his student's consternation. The work of a faculty member and administrator at a small liberal arts university never seems to end. Like Aelred, I cherish those quiet afternoons in my office when I can make time just to talk with my students, even if it means the guilt of putting my research and writing projects off for another day. After all, ought not the scholar who writes about friendship care first and foremost about such relationships?

As Plato's little *Lysis* dialogue presents, the practice of pedagogy in the communal search for wisdom is inherently a friendship endeavor. Writing a book, on the other hand, can be a lonely process. It also cannot be done without a community. I am thankful for the multiple undergraduate students at Pfeiffer University, the majority of whom were not majors, who explored together with

1. Aelred of Rievaulx, *Spiritual Friendship*, 69.

me the meaning of friendship in their third year seminars. They were a captive audience who patiently, sometimes excitedly, and often critically read drafts of these chapters. They were a wonderful sounding board for new ideas and theories. I am also thankful to my colleagues and friends at the Southeastern Commission for the Study of Religion/Society of Biblical Literature Southeast who heard drafts of these chapters as paper presentations throughout the years. I am thankful for the feedback and the space to explore my ideas deeper. I am also thankful to Elaine Heath and Larry Duggins of the Missional Wisdom Foundation for their vision of a renewed ecclesia in the twenty-first century, as well as the foundation's generous and creative partnership with Pfeiffer University. Finally, I thank most of all my wife Jana, my best friend, who has patiently endured my moods and frustrations as I carved out time away from her to write and edit. Without such a group of friends, this book could never have come to fruition.

Introduction

Friendship and Community in Contemporary United States, Ancient Greece and Rome, and the New Testament

WHAT DOES FRIENDSHIP LOOK like today? Who are our friends? Where do we find them? In spite of new technologies and increased mobility, are we lonelier than ever? Is friendship changing? Is friendship a virtue, merely beneficial to human flourishing, or an essential part of human life? These are not new questions. From the *Epic of Gilgamesh* to contemporary American TV series, narratives that reflect on the nature of friendship remain important to human culture. Anyone who watches TV can attest to the importance of friendship in the shows we like. From the popular *Cheers* in the 1980s to *Friends* or *Seinfeld* in the 90s and the more recent *Big Bang Theory*, viewers enjoy watching fictional characters pursue and develop friendships. One episode after another the characters in these stories meet in bars, coffee-shops, lunchrooms, and living rooms to do little except place one another in awkward, comedy-laden situations. Much may have changed since the *Epic of Gilgamesh*, but the human preoccupation with friendship has not.

While the plots of TV comedies are generally trivial, what is striking about them is that they reveal our continued desire for authentic and lasting friendships. TV viewers tune in to be "where everyone knows your name," as the theme song from *Cheers* goes. Such shows offer viewers not only the opportunity to reflect on the nature of friendship, they may also provide an escape. Reading or viewing the idyllic or flawed friendships of fictional characters may fill a kind of narrative void in our complicated, sometimes broken and hectic lives. Could it be that peoples' real lives are becoming so empty, so void of meaningful friendships and functioning communities, that the friendships portrayed in these television series provide at least a little reprieve from loneliness?

In his now classic *Bowling Alone*, Robert Putnam argues that there has been a serious increase in social isolation in America starting in the latter half of the twentieth century.[1] By compiling and analyzing numerous sociological studies, Putnam describes the decline of social capital, the "tangible substances that count for most in the daily lives of people": community, common cause, and social engagement and fellowship.[2] Among Putnam's most stunning findings were that informal social connections such as active involvement in clubs, visiting in one another's homes, and even having regular family meals were in measurable decline between 1970 and 2000.[3] Church involvement among younger people also slumped by at least 10–12 percent in roughly the same period.[4] These trends also impact individual lives and friendships. If friendship can be defined as discussing important matters with someone close to us, we may be in real trouble. McPherson et al. find that between 1985 and 2004 the sizes of average Americans' conversation networks have been shrinking. The number of people who

---

1. Putnam, *Bowling Alone*.

2. Putnam, *Bowling Alone*, 19.

3. Putnam, *Bowling Alone*, 93–115.

4. Putnam, *Bowling Alone*, 73.

report that they have no one with whom to confide has also tripled during this period.[5]

Such declines may also translate into the lives of religious communities. After a slight increase in the late '90s and early 2000s, the declines in church attendance have not only continued, but accelerated, with losses of between 11 and 18 percent between 2000 and 2010 among mainline Protestant denominations.[6] In addition, the sense of belonging one might derive from being part of a religious community has also decreased. The sample of Americans who had "no religion" in 1967 was at 2 percent. In the 1990s, this number had increased to 11 percent, with a full one in five reporting to the Pew Research Center that they had no religious affiliation in 2012.[7] If people are looking for community and friendship, it is increasingly less likely that they are seeking it in church.

The narrative that Americans are becoming increasingly socially isolated is not new. Numerous studies throughout the past century have looked nostalgically to a golden age of an idyllic past in American life, when friendships, communities, and families were still vibrant and healthy. Each succeeding generation of scholars and commentators has pinpointed different causes for disruption of friendships and community. Whether looking back in the 1930s to a pre-urban America, or looking back in the 1960s to an America that was not so highly industrialized, or looking back in the 1990s to an America before the era of the personal computer, there are those in each generation who look to the previous one to find conditions in which friendships and communities thrived.[8]

In assessing change, social scientists caution us from grasping easy answers. Putnam's work, as significant a contribution as it was, focused chiefly on Americans' participation in political, civic, and religious organizations, and other more traditional forms of work and social interactions. The way Americans are connecting

5. McPherson et al., "Social Isolation," 353–75.

6. Weems, "No Shows," 10–11.

7. Funk and Smith, "'Nones' on the Rise."

8. Wang and Wellman, "Social Connectivity," 1149.

is changing, but that doesn't necessarily mean a decline. True, Americans may no longer gather to play bridge as frequently as in the past.[9] However, with internet-driven social networking, Americans may have opportunities to connect and engage with people near and far over a myriad of interests. With the widespread adoption of the internet, Americans have seen measurable increases in the numbers and types of social connections online and beyond.[10] In fact, a summary of the data suggests that Americans may be able to count as many friends in the 2000s as in the 1970s, although the social contexts in which these friendships were made and sustained may have shifted from places like the church to the workplace or online.[11] Instead of seeing their social networks restricted to the Tuesday night neighborhood bridge club or the Wednesday night church supper, Americans might be using Facebook to find nearby running clubs or community bands. Perhaps they are networking through Instagram with photographers from all over the world, or connecting with an online weight loss website for support from dieters all across the country. Instead of becoming more socially isolated, in this global, technological age, many of us are more connected than ever.

Social scientists describe the new model in which people in the contemporary world relate to one another as "networked individualism." In such a world, "it is the person who is the focus: not the family, not the work unit, not the neighborhood, and not the social group."[12] This *reach beyond the world of tight groups* is what Rainie and Wellman describe as the first of a triple revolution that includes also an *internet revolution* of massively increased communication and information-gathering capacity, and a *mobility revolution* that allows us to experience "continuous presence and pervasive awareness" of others in the network, making physical

9. Putnam, *Bowling Alone*, 103.

10. Wang and Wellman, "Social Connectivity," 1164.

11. Fischer, *Still Connected*, loc. 904–7.

12. Rainie and Wellman, *Networked*, loc 337. Under title "Networked Individualism."

separation in time and space less important.[13] We are now part of social networks that are more geographically dispersed, more closely tailored to an individual's interests and pursuits, and provide people with new sources for solving problems and meeting personal and emotional needs.

The way we make friends and relate to communities is also shaped by changing demographic and economic factors. Claude S. Fischer, in his book *Still Connected: Family and Friends in America since 1970*, argues that vast changes in demographics and the economy have also contributed to a shift—but not necessarily a decline—in how Americans experience friendship and community.[14] For example, he points out that the average age in which both men and women get married has increased by about six years between 1970 and 2009. Likewise, people are waiting longer to have children, resulting in a larger number of twenty-somethings focusing on careers and dating, but not starting families. Overall, the population has aged, with fewer people in small rural communities, and more in socially disconnected suburbs. At the same time, because of a shifting economy, there are more married women aged 25–64 who are working, rising from 1 in 3 in 1960, to 2 in 5 in 1970, to 7 in 10 in the mid 1990s.[15] Such trends may contribute to the decline in the frequency of times that people sit down for family meals, visit neighbors' homes, or go to the club. On the other hand, women who otherwise might have been socially isolated in the home are now able to form new work friendships and build more extensive social networks. Contemporary single people in their 20s are likely to have larger friendship networks than their married peers of the '70s. More affluent families with both parents working longer hours may mean that families are having their meals and meeting others at restaurants, rather than visiting in neighbors' homes. Changing demographics and economy may

13. Rainie and Wellman, *Networked*. Chapter 1 under title "Triple Revolutions Impact," loc 442–450.

14. Fischer, *Still Connected*.

15. Fischer, *Still Connected*, chapter 1.

not mean an increase in social isolation, so much as the changing nature of friendship and community.

Organizations like the church that have tended to rely upon local community and tightly knit group allegiances are struggling to adapt to the challenges of networked individualism and these powerful shifts in demographics, economics, and technology. While the story of the demise of church and community may grab headlines, in a society of networked individualism, people are finding many new and creative ways of making friends, building community, and sustaining human contact. In light of the changing nature of friendship and community, with this book I hope to stimulate thought and discussion about how those of us who are shaped by a New Testament faith can reimagine our friendships, our lives together, and our communities.

We cannot reimagine what Christian community should look like in the coming century, unless we do a deep, biblical, and theological analysis of its roots in Christian friendship. Moses was viewed as a "friend of God" (Exod 33:1) while Jesus was scandalously viewed as a "friend of tax collectors and sinners" (Matt 11:19; Luke 7:34–35) in the Gospels. The ideal of Christian friendship, as reflected in various writings of the New Testament, had a markedly distinctive flavor in the ancient world. Among the philosophers of the ancient Greco-Roman world, friendship was a very important topic for the well-examined life. In fact, for some, like Aristotle, friendship was the chief virtue that someone could practice. It is my hypothesis that the New Testament writers used and adapted Greco-Roman friendship language, and transformed it to express the emergent experience of Christian community in their first-century Mediterranean world. As we examine transformed friendship language in the various New Testament writings, it is my hope that this book will contribute to the current discussion about new and emergent forms of Christian community in the twenty-first century. In each of the chapters below I will undertake a close reading of a passage or set of passages in which Greco-Roman friendship language is being transformed in one of the New Testament documents. I will then connect this passage with a contemporary context or issue that helps elucidate the distinctive way the New Testament authors have taken existing friendship language and transformed it to suit the needs of the emerging Christian community.

As I interpret these texts I shall be engaging a methodology called "narrative ethics" that I have been developing to read New Testament texts.[16] Narrative ethics conjoins the literary analysis of narratives with an examination of the ethical presuppositions represented within them, while considering how engaging such narratives might shape the moral imaginations of contemporary readers. Narrative ethics, therefore, proceeds on the *narratological*, *representational*, and *hermeneutical* levels.[17]

On the *narratological* level, narrative ethics examines the text closely for the kinds of story elements such as plot, character, point of view, etc. that a literary reading of a narrative might provide. Operating on the assumption that narrative form and function cannot be divorced, the narratological reading provides significant insight into how the narrator is shaping the moral imagination of the narrative audience, and hence provides us clues into how actual flesh-and-blood readers might appropriate or have their thoughts and emotions influenced by the text.

The second level, the *representational*, connects the narrative world with the cultural and social world in which the original flesh-and-blood audience is situated. Representational analysis operates on the assumption that language and its representations are critical in shaping the thoughts and culture of readers. Representational analysis, therefore, examines some of the philosophical and ethical assumptions common to the language communities that are engaging in writing and reading the narrative representations in the New Testament. Specifically, for this book, we will be examining how the New Testament writers are taking the philosophical and ethical assumptions apparent in the Greco-Roman

---

16. Hume, *Early Christian Community*, 23–40.

17. The nomenclature and three-part strategy for interpretation are borrowed from Newton, *Narrative Ethics*, 17–18.

expressions of friendship and representing these through characters and language that transform them in distinctive ways.

Finally, the third component of narrative ethics is called "hermeneutic ethics." Hermeneutic ethics examines how contemporary interpreters and readers might find themselves implicated by texts. In each chapter of this book, we shall use hermeneutic ethics to look to a contemporary community, experience, or issue. We shall also reflect on the ethical implications of reading and interpreting the individual passages that we thus examine. By examining the friendship language in each of the biblical passages chosen by this book, narrative ethics will connect the close reading of the passage to the moral imagination at play in a contemporary community, experience, or issue. How will that look concretely?

To understand how the New Testament writers shaped and changed the idiom of Greco-Roman friendship, it will be helpful to understand the significance of friendship in the writings of various Greco-Roman philosophers. The first chapter of the book, therefore, will provide a brief overview of friendship language in the writings of Plato, Aristotle, Cicero, and Plutarch.[18] For these ancient thinkers, human beings are social creatures; that is, human beings are made to live in the kinds of communities of friends that one might find gathered in the ancient Greek city state (Aristotle, *Eth Nic.* 1169b.16–21). For Aristotle and others, friendship was also considered a virtue, something that was achieved through a lifetime of practice (1098a.16–20), and that could only be reciprocated by equally high-status males (1156b.7–14; 1162a.34–1162b.5). Thus, friendship was considered a virtue that functioned as a social glue for the elite. Friendship provided the ethos for a loose network among the settled patriarchal aristocratic class that exercised political and cultural power. In fact, such friendship is grounded in love of self, as the friend was conceived of as

18. I'll be examining portions of Plato's *Lysis*, Aristotle's *Nichomachean Ethics*, Cicero's *Laelius: de Amicitia*, and Plutarch's "On Having Many Friends," and "How to Tell a Flatterer from a Friend." For this discussion, I'll be borrowing on some of the published findings of the Society of Biblical Literature's "Hellenistic Moral Philosophy and Early Christianity Group," as exemplified in Fitzgerald, *Friendship, Flattery, and Frankness.*

"another self" who in turn had also achieved moral self-fulfillment (1166a.30–34). As portions of Cicero's essay and Plutarch's treatise "How to Tell a Flatterer from a Friend" demonstrate, especially during the Roman period, men of high power are cautioned against flatterers who seek to exercise a kind of false friendship in order to gain favor. At least in these philosophical writings of the Greco-Roman world, friendship was considered a virtue of the elites, something that was practiced not only for a fulfilling and flourishing moral life, but also to provide a social foundation upon which the elites could exercise their power and privilege.

The New Testament transformation of the Greco-Roman friendship concept begins, of course, with Jesus himself. In the second chapter of this book we shall examine Jesus' saying, "the Son of Man has come eating and drinking, and you say, 'Look, a glutton and a drunkard, a friend of tax collectors and sinners!' Nevertheless, wisdom is vindicated by all her children" (Matt 11:19; Luke 7:34–35). First, the verse will be tested for its authenticity. Given its fit within an apocalyptic context, the references to John the Baptist in the verse's setting in both Matthew and Luke, and the fact that it would seem to shed a negative light on Jesus, it is quite likely that this is not only an authentic word of Jesus, but that it dates to one of Jesus' earliest sayings. What is more interesting is that it turns Greco-Roman friendship concepts on their head. Jesus' saying reinforces his repeated practice in the Gospels of embracing those who are despised and of low status. This is not the friendship of high-status elites. Introducing the sociological notions of group and grid developed by Mary Douglas, I shall show that Jesus' friendship practices shape a community of outcasts and misfits who have no place in a society in which there are high expectations of conformity and wide gulfs between elites and low-status individuals.[19] It is at this juncture that I turn to a discussion of how technology and social media have influenced the way we carry on friendships in contemporary society. The networked individual is no longer necessarily bound to relationships

19. Douglas, *Purity and Danger*; Douglas, *Natural Symbols*; Douglas, *Leviticus as Literature*.

with friends and family in one's immediate social and geographic circles. Facebook, Instagram, and other apps provide users the opportunity to connect with others all throughout the world, making it far easier to accumulate bridging social capital. We shall examine whether social media has turned us into people who interact with only those with whom we agree and have affinity, or whether it offers us the opportunity to connect with those outside of our social groups. Likewise, ISIS and other terrorist groups have taken to social media, using apocalyptic imagery and language to appeal to outcasts and misfits in Westerns societies while the gaps between social elites and the rest are increasing. The chapter concludes with some reflection on whether the church is missing an opportunity to make a friendship appeal through social media to the outcasts, broken, and lonely in today's world.

The third chapter examines the parable of the Good Samaritan in Luke 10:25–37. Looking at Jesus' command to "go and do likewise," the chapter concludes that the kind of friendship Jesus is talking about has to do with the experience of allowing oneself to be cared for by a stranger, becoming vulnerable like the man who has been beaten and robbed. This chapter takes as its contemporary focus the interdenominational organization Mission Mississippi, an evangelical nonprofit agency that formed in the 1990s to overcome deep racial divisions between African Americans and White Christians in the state of Mississippi. Mission Mississippi accomplishes its goals by fostering friendships among individuals, as well as forging partnerships and economic development opportunities between white and black churches. This chapter engages the work of Peter Slade's in-depth discussion of Mission Mississippi. Looking at the work of the nonprofit, Slade develops a "lived theology of friendship" in theological conversation with Jürgen Moltmann and Miroslav Volf.[20] My exegetical work in this chapter counters readings of the passage that view the Samaritan as the moral exemplar engaging others with acts of charity. Rather, I find that one can view the parable as a kind of "neighbor quest," an interrogative *midrash*, in which one imagines all facets of what it

20. Slade, *Open Friendship*.

would mean to give up trust in one's own socioreligious privilege, and become vulnerable, to receive compassion from a surprising lower status stranger. In other words, I show that, if anything, the exemplar in the parable is not the Samaritan, but the believing Jew who allows himself to be helped by the Samaritan. As I interpret this passage, reflecting particularly on Slade's discussion of Mission Mississippi and his use of Volf's concept of the embrace, I find that Jesus is teaching a friendship that practices a kind of "double vision." Our role is to see not only our own "will to embrace" the stranger, but to see and hear others' truths and claims for justice more strongly than our own.

The next chapter examines the passages in Acts that depict the early Christian community (2:41–47; 4:32–35). Luke writes narrative summaries that depict the early believers as "sharing all things in common" (2:44; 4:32) and "being of one heart and soul" (4:32). These aphorisms would have been instantly recognized by the ancient Greco-Roman audience as belonging to a *topos* on friendship that was widespread and well known in the writings of ancient antiquity.[21] In the immediately preceding context of these summaries, Peter's Pentecost sermon (Acts 2:14–40) accents the emotion of joy (2:25–26). Recognizing that ancient Greco-Roman moralists used emotions as part of their "moral therapy,"[22] I then turn to the summaries to see Luke describing the practices of the community as proceeding with joy (2:47). Indeed, one can make the case that joy is a significant narrative motif in Luke-Acts, a motif that reinforces a distinct ethical perspective in the intended audience.[23] This is one way in which the text intersects with contemporary contexts. Looking at the youth culture of contemporary North America, the sociologist Christian Smith has developed the concept of Moral Therapeutic Deism (MTD). MTD invokes a deistic god who has vaguely moralistic expectations while providing for its adherents' every emotional and physical need, what some

21. Johnson, "Making Connections," 159.
22. See Nussbaum, *Therapy of Desire*; Nussbaum, *Fragility of Goodness*.
23. See Inselmann, *Freude*.

have characterized as a "divine butler and on-call therapist."[24] As I explore and engage Smith's findings, I put my finger on a serious problem for our contemporary North American culture. We consume a salacious diet of increasingly predictable, contrived, violently titillating, and poorly conceived narratives. We hunger for authentic friendships and complex narratives. Perhaps stories and scenes like the one we find in Luke-Acts might sate that hunger. Stories that present human communities in relationship with a counterintuitive, creative, and joy-giving God challenge simplistic theological notions and inspire us to seek out authentic and surprising friendships.

The fifth chapter focuses on friendship language in the Fourth Gospel. In John 15:13, Jesus proclaims, "No one has greater love than this, to lay down one's life for one's friends." The particular saying that friends would lay down their lives for one another was well known in antiquity. It can be found in the writings of Plato (*Symp* 179B, 208D), Aristotle (*Eth. Nic.* 9.8.9), Seneca (*Ep.* 9.10), and even Paul (Rom 5:6–8).[25] By using this saying, Jesus is in some heady philosophical company. Greco-Roman philosophers repeated the claim that soldiers (as friends) lay down their lives for one another, and for a greater good. This provides the hermeneutical connection to contemporary concerns. Soldiers returning from wars in Iraq and Afghanistan are often heralded for their sacrifices for country. Indeed, a 2006 study found that one in eight recently returning wounded Iraq or Afghanistan veterans could be diagnosed with PTSD.[26] Other studies conducted in 2001 and 2003 found that approximately 31 percent of veterans from all wars suffer a lifetime prevalence of PTSD.[27] My reading of John asks not so much what John's teaching offers veterans, but what insights veterans can bring to the text. Veterans, who have known the stress and trauma of battle, may have a great deal in common with the Johannine community. John's Jesus shapes a community

---

24. Smith and Denton, *Soul Searching*.
25. See also O'Day, "Jesus as Friend," 149.
26. Taylor and Sherr, "When Veterans Come Home," 10.
27. Gradus, "Epidemiology of PTSD."

of insiders who have tightly woven friendships. Their community stands in stark contrast to a world that rejects Jesus. Veterans, who have gone through similar trauma, may indeed understand these statements by Jesus in ways that those of us who have not seen war cannot. The key difference is that Jesus' teachings lead to a community that dwells in peace (14:27; 16:33; 20:19, 21), a healing balm for vets with PTSD, and a hope-filled reality for all who follow Jesus.

The next chapter examines Paul's letter to the Philippians. When Paul calls on the Philippians to a *Koinonia* of the Spirit and to share the same mind and same love (Phil 2:1–2)—while recognizing them as equals in giving and receiving gifts (Phil 4:15)—he is using elements of the Greco-Roman friendship idiom.[28] My exegetical analysis focuses on the "Christ hymn" in Phil 2:6–11. In it, Paul praises Christ, who is equal to God, for taking on the form of a slave, taking on humanity's suffering, and indeed, becoming human himself. This notion of self-emptying ties into the contemporary foreground for this chapter, which is provided by the thoughts and writings of Jean Vanier, the founder of the international L'Arche movement, and 2015 winner of the Templeton Prize.[29] The L'Arche movement comprises approximately 150 communities of mentally disabled people and their live-in assistants throughout five continents.[30] These homes provide not only a dignified living environment for mentally and sometimes also physically disabled persons, they are organized as spiritual communities of friendship. Vanier's doctoral work, which was on Aristotle's friendship ideas, provides the philosophical and theological underpinnings for experiencing and expressing friendship, particularly with those who in some sense are viewed by society as misformed, and hence, throw away

---

28. For studies on Paul's use of the Greco-Roman friendship idiom in Philippians, see Malherbe, "Paul's Self-Sufficiency"; Peterson, "Philippians 2:5–11"; Reumann, "Philippians."

29. "Short Biography," *Jean Vanier: Transforming Hearts*, https://www.jean-vanier.org/en/meet-jean/biography.

30. "Short Biography," *Jean Vanier: Transforming Hearts*, http://www.jean-vanier.org/en/the_man/biography/short_biography.

objects.[31] Vanier claims that society can be transformed when we experience the kind of belonging that recognizes the vulnerability of others as an extension of our own brokenness—and nevertheless enter into tender relationship.[32]

Connecting to the themes of self-emptying and issues of disability, my analysis in this chapter looks at the Greco-Roman ideology of *kalokagathia*. Since the "good" and "beautiful" human form was thought to be that of the typical physically abled Greek or Roman male, less abled people, oftentimes slaves, were considered deformed not only physically, but also spiritually and morally as well. The chapter examines what it meant for friendship in the Philippian community to imagine a Christ for whom taking on the form of a human is equivalent to taking on the form of a disabled slave. I argue that Paul's use of reverse *kalokagathia* in this passage is the key to understanding contemporary friendship theologies like Vanier's. Friendship with those who are rejected by society is key to recognizing one's own vulnerabilities and becoming human.

The final chapter of biblical interpretation examines the letter of James. Starting from James's friendship language in 4:4, that "friendship with the world is enmity with God" and that "whoever wishes to be a friend of the world becomes an enemy of God," my examination focuses on what James means by friendship with the world. Throughout James's letter we see a kind of ethical dualism in which the author is rejecting elitist Greco-Roman friendship practices. With his notions about the reversal of wealth and poverty (1:9–11), his warnings against wealth (5:1–6), and showing favoritism toward the wealthy (2:1–7), James is basing his community ideal not upon sharing friendships with equally high-status males, as was the case of many of the authors of antiquity. Instead, he is setting forth a kind of rule of life for a community in which generosity (1:17), poverty (2:5–6), impartiality (2:1–4, 9), righteous action and teaching (1:22–25), and long-suffering (5:11) are encouraged and maybe even required. This rule of life shapes alternative community. Here, I will be in conversation with some

31. Vanier, *Made for Happiness*.
32. Vanier, *Becoming Human*, 57–62.

of the leading figures of a new movement to rethink community and church, new monasticism, by examining some of the work of Shane Claiborne, Jonathan Wilson-Hartgrove, Elaine Heath, and others.[33] New monastic communities are offering contemporary Christians ways of experiencing friendship that are alternative to the friendship offerings we find in much of contemporary society. They are also reimagining and reshaping the communal foundations upon which the church might be built. Such communities, therefore, are not only examples of the spirit of James, they take his alternative approach to heart.

The concluding chapter offers observations about a biblical theology of friendship and community. Just as Jesus and the New Testament writers grappled with the ways in which friendship and community were typically expressed in the first century, so also we are called to rethink friendship and community in the twenty-first century. What does a biblical theology of friendship look like in a world of networked individualism? How might a biblical theology of friendship address such issues as the need for narrative richness, racial reconciliation, care for those who have experienced trauma, or are living with disabilities? How might a biblical theology of friendship help us to imagine what life might look like in new monastic communities?

The New Testament writers took Jesus' boundary breaking friendship practices and transformed them into a way of life, incorporating them into the very structures of their community. They eschewed the practice of friendship among high-status individuals in which reciprocity in goods, favors, and kindness was expected. Instead, the New Testament writers practiced friendship with those who were least able or expected to give in return. This, of course, reverses social status and economic norms. Rather than calling them friends, the writers of the New Testament characterized their community members as "brothers and sisters" and of course, "believers," "who share all things in common." By incorporating Jesus' notions of fictive kinship and equalizing all under

33. Heath and Duggins, *Missional, Monastic, Mainline*; Heath and Kisker, *Longing for Spring*; Wilson-Hartgrove, *New Monasticism*; Duggins, *Together*.

God, the authors of the New Testament introduce the notion that the believers' primary friendship is with God. This vertical relationship transforms the quality and character of the horizontal friendships one has in spiritually infused Christian community. This transformation allows us to reconcile with former enemies, be in community with the disabled, broken, and traumatized, and set forth a new vision for community, story, and life in a world that is lonely, narratively deprived, and saddled with self-serving friendships.

2

Friendship in the Greco-Roman World

GREEK AND ROMAN THINKERS understood friendship as a defin-
ing characteristic of humanity, a virtue to be practiced, and an
important characteristic of citizenship. Numerous philosophers
of the Greco-Roman period place friendship at the center of
their discussions of what the ethical life should look like. Martha
Nussbaum, in her work on the Classical and Hellenistic periods,
characterizes the task of the Greco-Roman ethicist as a form of
therapy.[1] The moral life served the goal of human flourishing. The
task of the Greco-Roman moral thinker, therefore, was to provide
guidelines on what that flourishing should look like. In particular,
Nussbaum shows that moral philosophy of the period was to assist the student to appropriately channel and control desire. The
Stoics, for example, taught their students to frame and control
their desire in light of the more or less predetermined workings of
the divine *logos*. The Epicureans, on the other hand, taught how to
maximize pleasure while minimizing pain. The Greeks recognized
that friendship, at least in part, was about channeling human desire. Learning how to practice friendships properly, therefore, was
essential to a flourishing life in community with others. As such, it

1. Nussbaum, *Therapy of Desire.*

becomes the bedrock for a flourishing human society, for political activity, and the well-being of the state.

Plato

Desire and friendship are the topics of Plato's playful dialogue, *Lysis*. The dialogue opens with Socrates bumping into a group of young boys on the street, and walking with them to the wrestling school where they typically meet in the afternoon to play dice and exercise. As he walks with the boys, he discovers that one of them, Hippothales, has fallen in love with one of the other boys, Lysis. Hippothales apparently has made quite a spectacle of himself, writing love poems and love songs and talking about Lysis all the time (*Lys.* 203a–206c). Curious about who this Lysis may be, when they arrive at the *palaestra*, Socrates begins a conversation that attracts a circle of boys. Among them are Lysis, and Menexenus, Lysis's good friend. As the dialogue begins with Hippothales bashfully watching from the periphery, the topic quickly turns to the friendship between Menexenus and Lysis. In the meandering dialogue that follows, Socrates and the boys arrive upon multiple definitions of friendship.

Socrates begins by teasing the two boys, Menexenus and Lysis, by asking them who is older, better looking, of nobler birth, and richer. As he asks about their wealth, Socrates comes upon one of the commonly accepted definitions for friendship in the Greek world.[2] While the boys, as friends, may still compare themselves to each other in terms of wealth, beauty, or social standing, when it comes to possessions, "friends have all things in common" (207c). The phrase "friends have all things in common" was a kind of proverb in the Greco-Roman world. It can be found in multiple locations in the philosophical and ethical literature of the period. It occurs not only in works by Plato[3] and Aristotle,[4] but also in the

2. See also Grayling, *Friendship*, 20.

3. *Critias*, 110c; *Leges*, 739C; *Lysis*, 207C; *Phaedrus*, 279C; *Resp.*, 424A, 449C;

4. *Ethica eudemia*, 1137b, 1240b; *Eth. nic.*, 1159b; 1168b; *Magna moralia*,

works of Plutarch, [5] Cicero,[6] Seneca,[7] Philo,[8] Diogenes Laertius,[9] and Iamblichus,[10] to name only a few.[11] Given this widespread usage, we find variants of the proverb also in the New Testament, including in Acts 2:44 and 4:33, as well as alluded to in Philippians 4:10–20. Perhaps because the maxim was so widely accepted and known in the Greco-Roman world,[12] the boys readily agree with Socrates that they do not see any difference between them at all in wealth. Friends, after all, share all things in common. Eschewing his usual method here, Socrates does not question or dwell on the definition at all here. Of the various definitions for friendship that are considered in this dialogue, this is the only one that receives no further dialectical scrutiny. The boys portrayed in this dialogue clearly have leisure to spend their afternoons in the gymnasium. It is also clear from later portions of the dialogue that both Lysis and Menexenus come from families of great wealth and power. Since "friends have all things in common," the boys do not even consider their families' wealth an issue.

In the dialogue that ensues between Socrates and the boys, Plato makes an interesting connection between pedagogy and

---

2.11.49.5; *Politica*, 1263a;

5. *Amatorius*, 767D; *De amicorum multitudine*, 96f; *Cato minor* 73.4.3, (794D); *Conjugalia praecepta*, 143A; *De fraterno. amore*, 478D; 490E; *Marcellus*, 17.3.4; *Quaestionum. convivialum libri IX*, 644C; *Non posse suaviter vivi secundum Epicurum*, c. 22.4.

6. *Laeius*, 92; *De officiis*, 1.51; 1.56c.17.

7. *Epistula morales*, 48.2; *De beneficiis*, 7.4.1; 7.12.1.

8. *De vita Mosis*, 2.105.

9. *Vitae philosophorum* 4.53.8; 8.10.6; 10.11.6.

10. *De Vita Pythagorica*, 6.32.1; 19.92.21.

11. The list may include also Dio Chrysostom (*De regno* iii, 135R), Libanius (*Epistulae*, 1209.4.3;1537.5.2), Strobaeus (*Anthologium*, 4.1.161.11), Olympiodorus (*In platonis Alcibiadem commentarii* 88.12), Theophrastus (*Fragmenta*, 75.1.1), and Timaeus (*Fragmenta*, 3b,566,F.13b.2), as well as early Christian writers—often following the descriptions of Acts—Cassiodorus (*De anima* 517b), Clement of Alexandria (*Protrepticus* 12.122.3.1[94P]), et al.; See also Mitchell, "Social Function," 257; Bohnenblust, "Beiträge zum Topos Peri Filias," 40–41.

12. See also Johnson, "Making Connections," 159.

friendship. Socrates continues by questioning Lysis about his own power and self-determination. In a discussion that may remind a Christian reader of Gal 4:1–2, Socrates asks Lysis why his parents have placed him under the tutelage of slaves to be his tutors and teachers, if he is indeed so powerful. A high-status boy in the ancient world often would not have been allowed to exercise his power to do as he pleased. Instead, as a youth, his privilege enabled him to receive an education that lower-status boys would not have had access to. Through pedagogy, typically by slaves, he gained mastery in the various arts and skills needed to exercise power in his society. For Socrates, such pedagogy is a form of friendship. By pointing out the deficiency of the boy's knowledge, the goal of pedagogy is for the student to seek wisdom (210d–e). Wisdom, which can be defined as competency in such things as statecraft and the like, benefits those who possess it by attracting in turn other friendships and powerful connections. Nevertheless, it must be taught (210d). *Lysis,* as a dialogue, can at times be frustrating because its insistent Socratic analysis leaves so many of its friendship concepts unresolved. Still, we see a form of friendship being practiced in this dialogue. Socrates is "befriending" these boys by pointing out their deficiencies through targeted and relentless interrogation, all the while leading them toward wisdom. As such, the *Lysis* dialogue is a wonderful expression of the Socratic method as an active friendship practice.

After his discussion with Lysis, Socrates then proceeds through various definitions of friendship, deconstructing and discarding each one as he goes along. Socrates begins by asking whether the friend is the subject or the object of love (211d–e). He concludes that true friendship cannot exist if the friend is conceived of as the only one who is giving love. Likewise, the friend cannot be the only one who receives love. In some sense, friendship is only possible if it is reciprocated. He concludes that reciprocity has to be part of friendship.[13] However, it does not

---

13. The question of reciprocity in friendships will also be taken up later by writers in the Greco-Roman era, particularly Aristotle. Grayling claims that for Plato, mutual utility is the "founding principle of friendship" (*Friendship,*

take long for Socrates to pick apart the definition of friendship as reciprocity. For example, parents can still be seen to be friends of a baby, even (or especially) when the baby is crying and not reciprocating their love. Likewise, an enemy can be loved by someone and still be a friend. For example, for some of us, exercise may be experienced as an enemy. It does not necessarily love us back. Still, by consistently pursuing exercise, even if we at times experience it as an enemy, we receive rewards. For my students, especially in this attention-addled age, studying may be experienced as an enemy. Still, the love of and pursuit of such enemies has its own rewards.

After rejecting the definition of friendship as reciprocity, Socrates comes to the question of whether we are and can be friends with those who are naturally like us, in terms of virtue and self-sufficiency. Or, are we more likely to be friends to those unlike us? It would seem that like are indeed friends to like. However, as he proceeds, he realizes that those who are wicked cannot be friends with others, and certainly not with others who themselves are wicked (214c). From this, he concludes that only the good can be friends with the good (214d). However, this definition falls apart because those who are truly good are self-sufficient, and have no need of others. Hence, the truly good cannot be friends (214c–d).[14] From this irony, for at least a while, Socrates arrives at the conclusion that instead of like being friends to like, those who are opposites are friends to another (215e). However, he quickly dismisses this conclusion, because it is again readily apparent that the good cannot befriend the bad (216b–c).

The conclusion that Socrates arrives at is that "what is neither good nor bad is friend to the good" (217a). This is a difficult conclusion, but it also confirms Socrates's discussion on the relationship between wisdom, friendship, and pedagogy that he had with

---

25). I am not so certain. In my reading, Plato's discussion of friendship is more an illustration of the function of pedagogy. For Aristotle's disagreement that utility was the basis of friendship, see my discussion below.

14. In this discussion, Socrates places his finger on a problem that Aristotle and other later figures will also struggle with. Friendship in some sense always entails the experience of human need and desire. However, those who have needs and desires often do not make the best friends.

Lysis earlier. For Socrates, those who are already wise—whether gods or men—already love wisdom and have no need of friendship with the wise. Those who are fundamentally bad and ignorant see no need for wisdom; do not love it; and so will not seek it out. Wise friends are lost on those who are ignorant or bad. Only those who are aware of their own ignorance will seek out wisdom, finding wise friends to lead them on the journey. Since ignorance is a form of evil for Plato, the final definition to which Socrates arrives in the dialogue is that "The friend is friend of its friend for the sake of a friend, on account of its enemy" (219b). The logical problem with this definition is that it leads to an infinite regress. Here again is the problem of human desire and need. Those who seek out friendship, at least philosophical kinds of friendships, do so because of their awareness of some deficiency, some evil, some sort of ignorance within. Out of these deficiencies we seek out others who can help us. Those who do help us, we call our friends. These friends, however, befriend us for the sake of others, who in turn befriended them in their need, and so on in infinite regress. What we see at play here is the idealism of platonic philosophy. At some point, there is a need for an ideal friend, the perfect friend who possesses perfect wisdom, a kind of first principle that moves us, with our human deficits, toward friendship. But, as he pointed out earlier, the perfectly wise person would have no need of another, and ironically have no need of friends.

Pedagogy moves us toward human friendship, because it helps us to recover the good from our own desires. In this sense, Plato's moral and ethical answer to the question of friendship is therapeutic. For Socrates, desire is neither good nor bad. As humans, even when the bad is abolished, desire will continue to exist (221b–c). For desire, which is the cause of friendship, is rooted in the human need for completion, for the experience of that which is real, and the need for the highest good. Desire, therefore, is the seed of the ideal in the human soul. It is a striving for the good. Plato's therapeutic conception, his moral teaching about friendship, is that friendship is a pedagogical practice in a community of those who desire to experience wisdom and the highest good in their lives. However, for Plato, this ideal is ultimately not achievable. Socrates concludes that the good cannot truly be friends with the good, since those who possess the good in itself are self-sufficient. The truly good person has no need of others. Thus, the dialogue concludes with everything up in the air. At the very end, as the pedagogue slaves come to pick up their young charges, Socrates is looking around for someone older and wiser to help him out of the conundrum at which he has arrived. Friendship for Socrates is experienced in a company of seekers who are aware of their own deficits. In the Socratic community, friends look to one another to grow in wisdom.

Aristotle: Friendship as a Virtue

For many people today, friends are those with whom we like to spend time, or in whom we can confide, or on whom we can rely upon when we are going through difficult times. I wonder, though, whether many of us would define friendship as a virtue. Of course, whether we are entirely cognizant of it or not, we often apply ethical categories to our friendships. We expect reciprocity, honesty, and fairness from our friends. We also endeavor to be there for our friends when they need us. This certainly makes our friendships virtuous. How many of us, though, engage in the practice of friendship as a virtue all its own? This is precisely Aristotle's claim. For Aristotle, friendship is not only a virtue (*Eth. Nic.* 1155a.3–4), it is the chief virtue for political life, for experiencing a flourishing life in an ancient Greek city state.[15] The critical question we must ask is whether Aristotle's definition and understanding of friendship is reserved for an elite few, or whether it can be applied more generally.

15. See also Grayling, who connects Aristotle's reading of friendship in the Nichomachean Ethics to his Politics: "The *Nichomachean Ethics* precedes the *Politics* for good reason. 'Society depends on friendship' (1295b23–25), Aristotle says there. . . . He says, 'Philia is the motive of society' (1280b38–39) and that it is even more important than justice because it is what promotes concord in the city" (1280b38–39; Grayling, *Friendship*, 31–32).

Aristotle defined virtue as "a state involving rational choice, consisting in a mean relative to us and determined by reason" (1106b.35—107a.2). This definition of course needs unpacking. For Aristotle, the soul consists of three parts: feelings, capacities, and states. Aristotle recognized that human beings experienced feelings, or affects, as part of the flow of ongoing experience. As we discussed earlier, Greco-Roman moralists were providing "therapy" for the soul, and hence teaching humans how to engage or regulate their feelings. Aristotle names feelings that we too would recognize, such as appetite, anger, fear, confidence, etc. Capacity, the other part of the human soul, is that which makes us capable of experiencing feelings in one way or another. The state, then, is that part of the soul that enables us to be well or badly disposed toward our feelings. If the capacity of the soul is the battery that enables us to feel or generate emotions, so the state is something akin to a control switch.

According to Aristotle's definition, the state of one's soul cannot be considered virtuous unless it is regulated by rational choice. With the use of reason, and in accordance with a mean that is set relative to each individual's own capacity, our virtue allows us to control to what extent we can and ought to feel in any given situation. As he discusses virtue, Aristotle claims that our goal is to find the appropriate mean between two extremes of the same feeling. This will naturally differ for each person and each situation. The virtue of courage, for example, relates to how one moderates fear. The one who is overly fearful displays cowardice. The one who does not experience enough fear, on the other hand, will act in a foolish manner. As a virtue, courage is a state that involves rational choice to experience the proper measure of fear in a given situation. It will differ for each individual in accordance with each situation. The battle-tested and skilled soldier will use reason to measure his fear and react appropriately in a way differently from the soldier who is inexperienced and unskilled. As long as each is attempting what is appropriate to his level of experience and skill, they are practicing the virtue of courage.

With that in mind, we also see that honing the virtues requires a lifetime of practice. We change in our capacities over our lifetimes, and indeed are prone to react with different emotions to similar and varying situations over our lives. Our virtues, however, can be practiced and trained, so that we can rationally find the most suitable emotional fit for the situation in which we find ourselves at any given moment. Friendship, as a virtue, moderates between the extremes of being overly friendly and not friendly enough. On one end of the extreme one encounters obsequiousness (if there is no real reason for being friendly), or flattery (if one is seeking something from the other). On the other end of the extreme are people who are quarrelsome or peevish (1108a.27–31). One learns to train the virtue of friendship with the appropriate people in the appropriate ways over a lifetime of practice. For Aristotle,

> The human good turns out to be an activity of the soul in accordance with virtue, and if there are several virtues, in accordance with the best and most complete. Again this must be over a complete life. For one swallow does not make a summer, nor one day. Neither does on day or a short time make someone blessed and happy. (1098a.16–23)[16]

Three Kinds of Friendship

Is every friendship virtuous? This is an important question to ask because, unlike some of the other virtues, friendship involves reciprocity (1156a9–11). As rational agents, we do expect some return in our friendships. Because of this, friendships are sometimes wrought with vexing and complicated expectations. It would appear that some friendships are less virtuous than others. How might one claim, for example, that friendship among thieves is virtuous? Aristotle stipulates that there are three kinds of friendship, only one of which is truly virtuous. Some friendships are based

16. Unless otherwise noted, translations here follow Aristotle, *Nichomachean Ethics*, translated by Roger Crisp.

largely on utility. Such friendships, which Aristotle claims exists chiefly between older people, consists largely in the exchange of benefits between the partners. One might think of two politicians or two businessmen who engage in a friendship of utility by exchanging various favors or business advantages with each other. Likewise, Aristotle also describes friendships that are based upon the exchange of pleasure. Primarily seen among youth, friendships of pleasure last only as long as both partners are extracting some pleasure out of the relationship. Friendships of utility and pleasure, therefore, are necessarily fleeting and ephemeral. As soon as the benefits and pleasures cease to be exchanged, the friendships dissolve (1156a.11–16). Friendships of utility and pleasure are therefore imperfect and are to be distinguished from truly virtuous friendships, in part because the friend is being instrumentalized. In such relationships, the "friend" is not loved for his or her own good, but only because loving him or her brings one an advantage of one sort or another (1156a.11–13). Thus, for Aristotle, not all kinds of friendship are virtuous, as many are undertaken simply for the sake of utility or pleasure.

Virtuous friendships are undertaken not to procure some value from the other, but in order to affirm the other's intrinsic value. One engages in virtuous friendships when there is some resonance between one's own intrinsic goodness and the goodness of one's friend.

> Complete friendship is that of good people, those who are alike in their virtue: they each alike wish good things to the other insofar as they are good, and they are good in themselves. Those who wish good things to a friend for his own sake are friends most of all, since they are disposed in this way toward each other because of what they are, not for any incidental reason. So their friendship lasts as long as they are good and the virtue is an enduring thing. (1156b.7–14)

It follows, therefore, that virtuous friendships are only possible between people who themselves are morally complete, and wish their friends the good, solely for the sake of their friends.

Those who are bad prove incapable of engaging in virtuous friendships because they are only looking for some sort of benefit or pleasure from the other (1157a.18–20). Because of all these restrictions, only very few can actually achieve this true form of friendship.[17]

Reciprocity and the Self

For Aristotle, most human beings, if not all, are still essentially rationally self-interested. While it is noble to imagine someone who will provide benefits to others without any expectation of return, most human beings rationally will seek some sort of advantage for themselves (1162b.34–39). Aristotle is famous for conceiving the friend as another self (1166a.30–34; see also 1168b.1–8). Aristotle bases this conclusion on the notion that friends are "one soul." So, with whom could one better be "one soul" than with one's self? Therefore, one is "one's own best friend," because "one must love oneself most of all" (1168b.9–12). This of course sounds surprisingly modern. However, one must also temper this notion of self-regard with Aristotle's pragmatic understanding that friendship is not possible without community.

> For friendship is community, and as we are in relation to ourselves, so we are in relation to a friend. And, since the perception of our own being is worthy of choice, so is that of the being of a friend. This perception's activity arises in our living together, so that, as one would expect, this is what we aim at. And whatever being consists in for each, or whatever the end for which each chooses to live, is it this that they wish to pursue in the company of their friends. (1171b.33–1172a.4)

Even when practiced in community, however, truly virtuous friendships are difficult. That is because, by definition, virtuous friendships—as opposed to friendships of utility or pleasure—can only be practiced as long as both friends are at an equally high level

17. See also Grayling, *Friendship*, 33–34.

self-sufficiency. Yet they are also practiced with an expectation of return. When a virtuous friendship devolves into a friendship in which one or the other of the friends is being instrumentalized for utility or pleasure, complaints naturally arise. Thus, it proves difficult for there to be true friendship between those who are unequal. When it does occur, friendships of honor and benefaction may well ensue, in which "the superior person should get more honor, and the person in need more gain, since honor is the reward of virtue and beneficence, while gain is what ministers need" (1163b.2–5). However as the gaps in social status, wealth, power, or other markers of self-sufficiency widen, friendships between unequals become less and less likely, if not outright impossible. Aristotle therefore cannot conceive of friendships between humans and the gods, nor between kings and those of inferior status (1158b.32—1159a.3).

With the social stratification of the ancient *polis* in mind, for Aristotle and his well-educated audience, when "friendships among the good" are the only types to be virtuous, what is meant are friendships among older elite males who are of high status politically, economically, culturally, and of course, morally. Aristotle does not devote much time in his treatises to women.[18] Nor does he think that youth have developed the capacity in the virtues to practice true friendship. He is famous for asserting that the proper relationship between free and slave is one of tyranny.[19] Clearly, large portions of the population of ancient Greece are left out of Aristotle's analysis. Aristotle's moral theory may have a wider and more universal appeal. Everyone indeed struggles with how to moderate their feelings in day-to-day life. However, friendship, which Aristotle considers the chief virtue, would seem to be practiced only between male elites, or among the gods and kings, of the ancient Greek *polis*.

18. Nussbaum critiques Aristotle for disclosing little about friendships among women, in part because he devoted more scientific attention to studying the physical and psychological traits of shellfish than he did to women. Nussbaum, *Fragility of Goodness*, 370–71.

19. *Eth. Nic.* 1134b.9–18; 1060a.23–1661a.10.

Cicero

Cicero wrote *Laelius De Amicitia* in 44 BCE sometime during the six month period after the assassination of Julius Caesar in March. Like many of Cicero's other philosophical writings, the work is not overtly political in nature. *Amicitia*, the practice of making and maintaining friendships, was, then as now, an indispensable ingredient for political success. Whereas for Aristotle friendship was the theoretical basis for human flourishing in the *polis*, given Cicero's context it is hard not to hear in this dialogue a practical and applied philosophy of friendship.[20]

The historical background for the dialogue is, I think, deeply illuminating.[21] While Cicero was not directly involved in Brutus's and Cassius's conspiracy against Caesar, he certainly approved of their actions. He even chided them for not also having included the elimination of Marc Anthony in their plans. On October 31 of the same year in which Caesar is assassinated, Cicero receives a friendship entreaty in a letter from the young Octavian, Caesar's named heir, saying that he would like to take up the republican cause. Perhaps hoping to split Anthony and Octavian, Cicero backs Octavian, while writing a series of "Philippics" against Anthony. As long as the two are fighting against another, he reckons, there may be a chance yet for the republic to be delivered. For a while his plan seems to work, until Octavian and Anthony align, splitting power between themselves and unleashing a proscription on which Cicero's name lands, chiefly because of his enmity with Anthony. Cicero must have known that his friendships with the republican plotters, while at the same time backing Caesar's heir against Anthony, could lead him into a dangerous spot. Whether he was aware that this would lead to his assassination within a year of writing this dialogue, of course, cannot be known.

20. "It carries the weight of Cicero's experience as a public man, and the plausibility of real historical examples which his contemporary readers knew and could judge." See Grayling, *Friendship*, 43.

21. For a lovely and very readable biography of Cicero, see Everitt, *Cicero*.

Given this context, it makes sense that Cicero lays down a basic law for friendship. One must not ask a friend to do something wrong, nor do anything unlawful or treasonable, if a friend should ask one to (*Amic.* xii.40). Indeed the elderly Cicero claims that there is a duty to teach those who might be caught up in such friendships that they are not duty bound to honor them (xiii. 44). That Cicero has a certain political context in mind for this advice is clear. Although the advice is given by the aged Laelius in his dialogue, one cannot but help to hear the clarity of Cicero's voice in his own political context.

> And so a community of interest with wicked men like these must not be glossed over by the plea of friendship; rather it must be suppressed with every stern measure at our command, so that no man may deem it lawful to stand by a friend even when he bears arms against his country. And this, by the way, is altogether too likely to happen, the way things are going. For my own part, I am no less concerned with the way the government will be after my death than with the way it is today. (xiii.43)[22]

Whether Cicero here is thinking of an armed Anthony and those who might align themselves with him, or has in mind Octavian who at the time of his writing was busily arming himself for a confrontation with Anthony and eventual march on Rome, we cannot be certain. Nevertheless, fidelity to law and constitution trump whatever political obligations friendship may require of one. Hence, his first law of friendship is "that we ask of our friends what is honorable and do what is honorable for the sake of our friends" (xiii.44).

As part of this political practice of friendship, Cicero advises several aspects. Friends should exercise their personal influence to provide frank advice to their friends, hence protecting them from corrupting influences (xiii.45). Likewise, as we saw in the case of Aristotle, friendships that are practiced merely for the sake of protection and assistance, with "freedom of care" as their goal, are not considered virtuous (xiii.45–47). Indeed, sometimes one

22. Translations follow Cicero, *On Old Age*, translated by Frank O. Copley.

must suffer on the behalf of one's friends, especially if it is to be demonstrably virtuous (xiv.49). While Cicero, as we saw above, advises against forsaking what is dishonorable in one's friendship expectations, he makes concessions for a certain practicality in friendships. As long as one shares an unblemished character with one's friend, and as long as there is complete transparency among friends in their concerns, plans, and aims, there may be occasions when one could be obliged to assist friends in aims that are not entirely commendable, as long as such aims involve life and death and or good reputation (xvii.61). In the tumultuous time toward the end of the Republic in which Cicero is writing his dialogue, one can imagine that Cicero made multiple such concessions on behalf of his friendships with one party or another. Surely this would have been the background for his observation that "it is very hard to discover true friendships among men who are engaged in politics and affairs of state" (xvii.64). Cicero's recent experience of Caesar's assassination, in which his body lay on the Senate floor after being stabbed multiple times by his conspirators, surely shades his observation of the friendless tyrant.

> This is how tyrants live—a life in which, as you well know, there can be no charity, no lasting assurance of the goodwill of men; always and everywhere there is suspicion and insecurity. No place for friendship here! Think! Who could love the man he fears, or the man who, he thinks, fears him? Tyrants are, to be sure, the objects of men's devotion, but it is all show and expediency. For if they should chance to fall, as frequently happens, it then becomes clear how poor in friends they are. (xv.52)

Apart from the political observations, Cicero's observations on friendship are not terribly original, derived as they are from previous Greek thinkers. Nevertheless, his definition of friendship as "complete sympathy in all matters of importance, plus goodwill and affection," has outsized influence on the later tradition of the medieval period. Medieval scholars were reliant upon Cicero, likely because his Latin manuscripts were more accessible than those of Aristotle and other Greek thinkers on friendship. As with

Aristotle, for Cicero friendship is based upon virtue (vi.20) and is universally essential (vi.22). Important for the later tradition is that, like Aristotle, Cicero does not trace the roots of friendship to mutual advantage. Instead, in a kind of nominalist argument, Cicero argues that friendship has its roots in inclinations of the heart, as *amor* is the root of *amicitia* (viii.27). As such, in friendship, the inclination of the heart is toward virtue, "For there is nothing so worthy of love as virtue, nothing that offers a stronger incentive to affection. Consider only the fact that we feel a kind of love even for men whom we have never seen, simply because of their virtue and probity." With such claims as this, connecting friendship to love, virtue, and the heart, it is hardly surprising that Cicero would be held in such high regard by later Christian thinkers.

In the end analysis, Cicero's discussion of friendship does not add much original to earlier Greek thought. His portrayal of the virtuous and self-sufficient man as the best at making and keeping friends differs little from Aristotle's understanding of the fully good man who practices friendship for the sake of virtue alone. What is interesting and distinctive in Cicero is the political context in which he writes this dialogue, perhaps the last of his philosophical works before his own assassination. His observations of the friendless tyrant and his warnings about the difficulties of maintaining friendships in the midst of political turmoil prove valuable for contemporary thinkers. David Brooks, the contemporary political thinker on friendship, writes a wonderful essay on the friendless Donald Trump on the campaign trail.[23] Clearly such dynamics continue to this day.

Plutarch

Plutarch, who lived from 46–120 CE, was a Middle Platonist whose essays on morality include a few pieces on friendship. A contemporary of second generation Christians, some of whom may have been responsible for the later writings of the New Testament or the

---

23. Brooks, "Donald Trump's Sad, Lonely Life."

earliest writings of the Early Church, his writing and thought prove instructive for understanding how the world of the Roman empire would have shaped their thinking and morals. Plutarch's two essays on friendship, "On Having Many Friends" and "How to Tell a Flatterer from a Friend," demonstrate the continuing significance of the practice of friendship as a virtue in the Roman imperial period. As we saw above, Aristotle's understanding of friendship is as a political virtue, in the sense of contributing to a thriving human community. Cicero's understanding of friendship, it could also be argued, was political, but practiced for self-preservation or advancement in the late Roman Republic. By the time we get to Plutarch in the late first/early second century, we are dealing with an imperial setting in which friendship must bend and adapt to the forces of hierarchical patronage in a society in which personal status is determined by honor.

One of the difficulties that readers of first century documents such as the New Testament have is to overcome the cultural assumptions we might bring to bear on a text as inhabitants of a hyper-capitalistic and hyper-consumerist world in which the primary means of exchange and accumulation is money. Wealth and its accumulation were, of course, important for some in the Roman imperial period. For most, though, higher levels of status were achieved through the accumulation of honor through a system of patronage and benefaction. Patrons received honor for various forms of benefaction. Those who received benefactions from patrons were in various ways beholden to them, owing them honor, fidelity, and in some cases, friendship. In a city or household of the Roman imperial period of the late first century, there was a great deal of social stratification based upon various markers of status. While it may have remained true, as for Aristotle, that friendship was ideally practiced between two equally high-status males, by the time we get to the late first century, unequal friendships, such as those described by Aristotle as friendships of utility, were more and more frequently being practiced. A high-status person, therefore, could, for example, expect "friendship" and reverence from large numbers of people by engaging in a large scale benefaction, such as a public works project, or by sponsoring chariot races or gladiatorial games. As we shall see with Plutarch, the widespread practice of patronage and benefaction in a highly stratified society can make friendships complicated.

Contemporary users of social media can perhaps readily appreciate the desire to accumulate many friends. In Plutarch's day, the accumulation of multiple friends would have demonstrated a high level of patronage, and hence status. In his essay "On Having Many Friends," Plutarch argues against the acquisition of many friends. He offers multiple arguments. His primary argument is that the craving of many friends is "antagonistic" to the acquisition of true friendship (2.1). Even though one might classify him as a middle Platonist, Plutarch's definition of true friendship differs greatly from Plato's ideal. Plutarch claims that friendship should be tested through three measures: "virtue as a good thing, intimacy as a pleasant thing, and usefulness as a necessary thing" (94 C–D).[24] What is curious is that he includes friendships of utility and pleasure, types of friendship that Aristotle clearly thought of as not belonging to the ideal. Because he includes more instrumental forms of friendship in his analysis, Plutarch claims that one cannot or should not have many friends. Multiple friends with diverging interests and needs can tear one into pieces. He is operating with a picture of the real life activities of friends in late first century who are

> occupied in diverse activities and experiences, and call upon us at the same instant, one to join him on a voyage to foreign parts, another to help him in defending a suit, another to sit with him as judge, another to help him in managing his buying and selling, another to help him celebrate his wedding, another to mourn with him at a funeral. (6.1–4)

Note how he describes these friendships more or less as the exchange either of various kinds of service of assistance, or as the exchange of emotion and solidarity.

---

24. Plutarch, *Moralia*, translations by F. C. Babbitt.

In this essay, Plutarch describes true friendship not so much in the terms of an abstract Platonic ideal, but as a "thoroughgoing likeness in characters, feelings, language, pursuits, and dispositions." The ideal friend, therefore, is steadfast in character, location, and intimacy. For this reason, Plutarch cautions against having many friends. Instead, in a world as stratified and busy as the late first century Roman Empire, the ideal is to find a single friend who can and will share in one's virtue, intimacy, and needs over the long run.

In an age of superficial social media friendships, my students surprisingly find Plutarch's essay "How to Tell a Flatterer from a Friend" particularly relevant. In it, Plutarch is giving advice to a high-status person, the kind of person who would attract many flatterers, or false friends. Flattery is a particularly dangerous and deceptive form of friendship, contends Plutarch, because it uses self-love as a springboard. Recall that Aristotle bases friendship in self-love. For Plutarch, this gives the flatterer tremendous room to maneuver, because of his ability to stoke self-deception and ignorance regarding what is truly good or bad for one's self. Flatterers seek out the powerful and ambitious and attach themselves to them as leeches: "but flatterers proclaim that kings and wealthy persons and rulers are not only prosperous and blessed, but that they also rank first in understanding, technical skill, and every form of virtue" (58E). For those who are powerful and high in status, learning to discern between flatterers and friends is an important skill. It is based in an understanding of what true friendship is. Part of the definition involves frankness. The true friend exercises a virtuous practice of frank speech, telling truths to the friend that the friend needs to hear—but may not want to. Plutarch advises that the friend should employ frankness at the proper time (66B), with respect, tact, and reverence, clear of personal feeling (67B), with an aim toward seeking good, even it if may be painful to hear (66E), and not done publicly. It may sometimes be a thankless task, "for it is the duty of a friend to accept the odium that comes from giving admonition when matters of importance and of great concern are at stake" (73). Powerful people of any era would be wise to surround themselves with true friends who speak bold and sometimes unpleasant truths. Woe be the ruler (and their subjects) who surround themselves only with flatterers who tell them what they want to hear. As my students move on to take positions of leadership in their communities and lives, Plutarch's advice is as timely as ever.

Conclusion

Greek and Roman philosophers valued friendship as a virtue. Although Plato's *Lysis* does not offer a conclusive definition of friendship, the dialogue illustrates that the ultimate outcome of the Socratic pedagogical practice was friendship. This notion, that friendship could be taught, learned, and practiced as a virtue, underlies all later Greek thinkers. For Aristotle, friendship becomes the chief virtue that one must practice for civic and public life. Unlike friendships of pleasure or utility, true friendship, as Aristotle discusses, is practiced only by a few who have reached the pinnacle of wisdom. For Aristotle, true friendship is grounded in self-awareness and love of self, but is practiced always reciprocally among those who were of the highest status. It is no surprise then that later Roman thinkers would pick up on friendship as a virtue that was useful for political life. For Cicero, friendship was a guiding force for those who engage in public life. In Plutarch's view, the ruler could only have a handful of true friends. Those who were the ruler's friends also never shied away from speaking honest and hard truths. Such true friends were to be valued over flatterers.

As we move toward a discussion of how New Testament writers engaged Greco-Roman friendship thought, there are three important aspects of the discussion to keep in mind. First, we must not lose sight of the Greco-Roman notion that friendship was indeed a virtue. As such, the practice of friendship was thought to be normative to the lives and communities of the Greco-Roman writers and audience of the New Testament. When the New Testament writers take up the language of friendship, they are self-consciously engaging language that has ethical and moral overtones. Friendship language in the New Testament, therefore, has normative connotations as well; although the friendship norms and morals reflected in the New Testament may differ from their Greco-Roman antecedents and near contemporaries.

Second, the virtue of friendship had clear communal, and indeed, political consequences. The New Testament writers use Greco-Roman friendship language to outline the shape of community, polity, and expectations for the common Christian life. Finally, we must be aware that the Greco-Roman philosophers (at least those whose treatises survived antiquity) were really only interested in discussing the kinds of friendship virtues that were practiced among high status elite males in their society. As Aristotle's analysis showed, true friendship among those who were not the elite, or among those who were young, or morally flawed, was not conceived to be possible at all. As we shall see, Jesus' friendship practices flipped this notion on its head, as he embraced the accusation that he was a drunkard and a glutton, a friend to tax collectors and sinners.

3

Gluttons, Drunkards, Tax Collectors, and Sinners

Jesus' Countercultural Friendships and Networked Individualism (Matt 11:19; Luke 7:34–35)

THE DISTINCTIVE NEW TESTAMENT notion of friendship likely has its source in the teachings and practices of Jesus and his earliest followers in the Palestinian context. The Gospels present Jesus and his followers as an itinerant movement that is dependent upon the finances and hospitality of various supporters, some of whom were women (Luke 8:1–3). The movement practiced friendship with folk who may have been considered as less than savory company by higher-status elites or those associated with the religious hierarchy. Jesus himself, in his discourse comparing himself to John the Baptist, admits as much. Recorded in Matt 11:19 and Luke 7:34, Jesus claims that those who oppose his ministry also opposed the ministry of John the Baptist. He also says that they call him "a glutton and drunkard, a friend of tax collectors and sinners." In much of contemporary scholarship there is little doubt that this is likely an authentic Jesus *logion*.[1]

1. For an extensive bibliography and listing of commentators who argue

The *logion* also confirms the depictions of Jesus' commensality and friendship practices in much of the rest of the Gospels. We see Jesus consistently dining and associating with the poor, marginalized, disabled, and broken. In a society in which power and honor were concentrated in small pockets of elites, Jesus, in a countercultural move to much of Greco-Roman society, sought the friendship of outcasts and undesirables.

Q 7:34 in its Apocalyptic Context

Matt 11:16–19 and Luke 7:31–35 relate a Q saying that likely dates back to Jesus' own words. The text is replicated in parallel in the NRSV below:

MATTHEW	LUKE
16 But to what will I compare this generation?	31 To what then will I compare the people of this generation, and what are they like?
It is like children sitting in the marketplaces and calling to one another,	32 They are like children sitting in the marketplace and calling to one another,
17 "We played the flute for you, and you did not dance; we wailed, and you did not mourn."	"We played the flute for you, and you did not dance; we wailed, and you did not weep."
18 For John came neither eating nor drinking, and they say, "He has a demon";	33 For John the Baptist has come eating no bread and drinking no wine, and you say, "He has a demon";
19 the Son of Man came eating and drinking, and they say, "*Look, a glutton and a drunkard, a friend of tax collectors and sinners!*"	34 the Son of Man has come eating and drinking, and you say, "*Look, a glutton and a drunkard, a friend of tax collectors and sinners!*"
Yet wisdom is vindicated by her deeds.	35 Nevertheless, wisdom is vindicated by all her children.

for the *logion*'s authenticity, see the discussion in Witetschek, "Stigma of a Glutton," 138–41.

Without getting into the details of how one reconstructs the actual text of Q, one can see that the saying has three parts.[2]

In the first part Jesus asks to what he should compare the people of this generation. He then answers his question by comparing the people of this generation to children in a marketplace who are unmoved and unimpressed by those who have come to entertain them or engage them in mourning. They do not dance for the flute player. They do not mourn with those who are wailing for the recently deceased. The word γενεά refers to an end-time audience that is unresponsive to apocalyptic appeals. Recurring throughout the synoptic Gospels, we see γενεά figuring prominently in the narrative contexts following the friendship *logia* in Matt 11:19[3] and Luke 7:34.[4] In the second part of the saying, Jesus describes himself and John as those who alternately call on the generation of the end of times to weep or dance. John, who fasted and did not drink wine, was said to have a demon. Jesus, who eats and drinks with his friends, is called a glutton and drunkard, a friend of tax collectors and sinners. The final part of the Q text likely included the wisdom saying, "wisdom is vindicated by her deeds/children." The rejection of Jesus and the argument that he associates with undesirables therefore is being forwarded by those who reject his apocalyptic message.

The Authenticity of the Text

From these contours of the Q saying, we can see that Jesus is commenting about his and John's reception among his peers in first century Palestine. The saying is likely authentic to the historical Jesus. As such it provides significant insight not only into Jesus' practice, but also how he viewed his practice in contrast to socially acceptable norms of his society. Those investigating the historical Jesus employ three basic tests for authenticating sayings attributed

2. See also Witetschek, "Stigma of a Glutton," 141.

3. Matt 12:39, 41, 42, 45; 16:4; 17:17; 23:26; 24:34.

4. Luke 9:41; 11:29, 30, 31, 32, 50; 16:8; 17:25; 21:32.

to the character of Jesus in the Gospels to the historical Jesus: independent/multiple attestation, historical and contextual conformity, and dissimilarity to the expectations (embarrassment) of later tradition.

Independent Attestation

The exact Q saying itself does not pass the criterion for independent attestation. Both Matthew and Luke appear to be using the same source, Q, for their context. The specific saying that we find in Luke 7:34 and Matt 11:19 thus is not repeated in any other text of early Christianity. However, other textual traditions do attest to the contrast between the practices of John and Jesus, while highlighting Jesus' commensality with undesirables and celebratory habits. Mark 2:14–22 presents Jesus having a meal with Levi the tax collectors, in which the Pharisees complain of Jesus' commensality with "tax collectors and sinners." Also here there is a question by Jesus' opponents about the contrasting practices of Jesus, who is eating and drinking almost in a celebratory fashion like a bridegroom, and John, who is fasting (Mark 2:18–19). Even John confirms Jesus' practice of celebratory commensality (John 2:1–13). So, while the specific Q text found in Luke 7:34 and Matt 11:19 is not attested in multiple texts, enough common elements of the text are attested both in Mark and John to argue for it being an authentic part of Jesus' typical ministry.[5]

Conformity

The second criterion for authenticity confirms or denies whether the saying's phrasing and content conforms to what we know about the historical and social realities of first century Palestine. In other words, could this saying have emerged authentically from

---

5. As Witetschek aptly summarizes, "The criterion for multiple attestation is more useful for determining characteristic behaviors of Jesus than for authenticating particular sayings." Witetschek, "Stigma of a Glutton," 141.

the world in which Jesus lived and acted? By turning its focus on the social world of first century Palestine, the third quest for the historical Jesus has provided considerable context for understanding Jesus' sayings and deeds. Under a mixture of Roman direct rule and control by Herodian client kings, a picture is emerging of a Palestine whose elites took part and were swayed by the culture and economics of Roman imperial power, while also breeding seething resentment against it among large swaths of the Jewish populace.[6]

The context in which John's and Jesus' movements emerge was one of vast social inequities. Historical studies point to a heavy burden of double taxation upon the populace of Palestine, with large numbers of landless peasants and day laborers scratching by however they could. Tax collectors and others aligned with the elite would have been vilified for exploiting the economic and political system to their advantage. On top of the status pyramid would have been the Roman retainer class, the Sadducees and other elites, who would have benefited the most from exploitation of those at the bottom. Many Palestinian peasants on the bottom of the social pyramid would have hoped for the restoration of a messianic kingdom in which they could see a reversal of social and economic justice along the lines of the Hebrew prophets. Luke 7:31–35 and Matt 11:17–19 present John and Jesus as populist leaders of related movements whose aim it was to restore an apocalyptic vision of Israel's national purpose and identity in a perceived eschatological context. Using the marketplace as a metaphor, Jesus is contrasting his style of presenting this vision with that of his predecessor, John. Whereas John's call was to fasting, repentance, and prophetic urgency, Jesus' is to boundary crossing commensality and celebration that God is about to renew God's covenant and enact an eternal kingdom among the people of Israel.

Jesus' movement, therefore, seemed to occupy a space between the social elites and the outcasts. On the one hand, by promising a divinely restored kingdom in which status and wealth

6. For a simplified discussion in compact form see Horsley, "Jesus and Empire," 44–74.

would have been reversed, and social and personal ailments would have been healed, the Jesus movement bridled the prophetic hopes and dreams of those who were socially displaced or on the lowest rungs of the Palestinian hierarchy. So, Jesus enjoyed solidarity and commensality with those regarded as social outcasts and sinners. On the other hand, by populating his movement also with tax collectors like Matthew and Zaccheus, Jesus likely did receive some financial and material support from those who had previously exploited the system to their own personal advantage, and maybe even were continuing to do so. This of course likely garnered some resentment among those both within and outside of his movement who might have been more radically aligned with those who were socially and economically marginalized. Jesus as "friend of tax collectors and sinners" may well capture both internal and external critiques of his movement practice. Jesus' description of the practices of his and John's movements and the way he depicts his critics cohere well with what we know from a thick description of the social context of first century Palestine. Jesus' saying very much passes the second test for historical reliability, the test of conformity to the social world of first century Palestine.

Dissimilarity or Embarrassment

The third test for historical authenticity, dissimilarity, seems to contradict the second test, conformity to what we know about the history and society of first century Palestine. The test of dissimilarity accounts for possible distortions that might occur through the later transmission of Jesus' sayings from an original Aramaic linguistic and rural Palestinian context to the more urban and Greco-Roman context in which the missionary proclamation of the expanding religious movement might have occurred. The hypothesis is that if the saying preserves something that is dissimilar to later contexts, it is more likely to have been distinctive to this earlier period. This is why this criterion is also sometimes called the criterion of "embarrassment." While later traditions may have been embarrassed by the saying, they retained it because of their knowledge of its authenticity. As the early Christian missionaries translated and transcribed Jesus' sayings from a rural Aramaic context to an urban Greek context, they were more likely to have tweaked or changed Jesus' sayings to conform to the expectations of this latter audience. If Jesus' saying has something that veered from the expectations of this latter audience, especially if it can be viewed as controversial or even confrontational, it is likely to be more original to the historical Jesus. As Q came to be written and used as a collection of Jesus' sayings, it naturally needed to take into account the needs of the developing churches in the larger cities of the Mediterranean. When one finds a saying of Jesus that contrasts with the later expectations and needs of a largely Gentile and Greek speaking audience, it is more likely to originate with the historical Jesus.

Jesus' saying, especially in Matt 11:19 and Luke 7:34, does pass the test of dissimilarity. The opponents' claims about Jesus' friendships hardly cast a charitable light on Jesus. It is hard to imagine later tradents having a missionary purpose in passing down material in which Jesus' opponents were claiming he was "a glutton and drunkard, and a friend of tax collectors and sinners." They must have done so only because they thought it somehow unavoidably linked to what people knew about Jesus already. For a study on friendship, however, the saying proves even more controversial than just the connection with gluttons, drunkards, tax collectors, and sinners. If one examines closely Greco-Roman moral philosophy on friendship, one sees that there are clear expectations connected to the kinds of people with whom one would befriend.

Friend to Tax Collectors and Sinners, not the Elite

Aristotle, as we have discussed, describes friendship as being possible between two equally virtuous high status males. Friendship between those who are not equally good, he claims, will naturally devolve into friendships of utility or pleasure. He is quite clear. The higher status individual only participates in friendships with lower status people to reap honor in exchange for the kinds of material favors he is capable of doling out. It is hardly surprising, therefore, that Aristotle claims there can be no true friendship between the gods and human beings. To be clear, I am not claiming that the Greco-Roman audience to which early Christian missionaries were appealing would have been familiar with Aristotle. However, in that they participated in a culture of patronage and status, for the Greco-Roman audience the depiction of a divine individual having friendships with undesirables without the requirement of honor being exchanged in return would not only have been "dissimilar," but rather shocking and embarrassing as well.

Appealing to Isolates in the End of Times

So what was the historical Jesus up to, then, in making friendships with undesirables? More importantly, how and for what theological purpose was this practice of Jesus' transmitted and shared in the next generation Gospel accounts? The historical Jesus was building an apocalyptic movement in preparation for the restoration of the Kingdom of God in the end of times. To be successful, Jesus' revolutionary movement needed to attract those who were most likely to be displaced by the social dynamics of the hierarchical society of first century Palestine, as well as those who were able to support his movement financially. Sinners and tax collectors would both be considered social isolates, while tax collectors would have had the financial wherewithal to support Jesus' movement. Jesus appealed to those who were for one reason or another misfits in a society that had uniformly shunned them.

Group and Grid in Different Societies

Mary Douglas proposes the concepts of group and grid to describe various facets and types of social organization.[7] Group describes

7. She lays out the notions of group and grid in relationship to ancient Israelite society and its practice of ritual purity. Given that the second temple played a huge role in first century Palestine, the concepts of group and grid can also be applied to this society as well. See Douglas, *Purity and Danger*.

the amount of social cohesion that a society may demonstrate. Societies with a high group factor are those in which various beliefs, cultural values, and ideas are commonly held among all or most of the members of society. Societies with a low group factor are those in which there is a diversity of viewpoints, social and cultural values, and ideas. Societies that have a high grid exhibit a highly structured differentiation between those with high status, the hierarchy, and those who have low status. Societies with low grid, on the other hand exhibit more egalitarian structure. Group and grid are very useful in describing various societies, as well as the social location within those societies.

If we lay down the grid, we find that we see four different kinds of society described. Individualistic societies, like the one in contemporary North America, are those in which there is low group and low grid. Of course, wealth has led to some social stratification in our highly capitalistic society, and there is vast diversity in values and beliefs. Nevertheless, most Americans still share at least some common commitment to egalitarianism. Each person has a vote. Groups and individuals have the freedom to worship as they feel moved. Most all Americans share the idea that anyone, with enough hard work and luck, can be successful. Sects, cults, and other kinds of enclavist groups are examples in which there is low grid and high group. All the members of the group share to a large degree a common commitment to a single set of values upon which they all believe. However, with the exception of the leader, most sects see relatively little social differentiation among the members. Societies in which there is a high grid but low group are those in which there is clearly a hierarchy, but also a wide range of values, beliefs, and ideas. Indian society, with its distinct classes and castes, might be a good example of a society in which there is high social differentiation, while also preserving a wide variety of religious expressions, diversity of beliefs, and philosophical and political commitments. Societies in which there is high grid and high group are those in which there is a strong commitment to a single set of values and beliefs, while maintaining a strong role for differentiation in terms of status and roles. Medieval Europe,

Imperial China, and Czarist Russia are societies that had distinct separation between aristocracy and peasants, with one pervasive worldview that was shared by all in their respective society: the doctrines of the Catholic Church in Europe, Confucianism in China, or the theology and practice of Eastern Orthodoxy in Russia.

First Century Palestine as High Group, High Grid Society

The society of first century Palestine also can be described as high group and high grid. While different groups within first century Judaism may have disagreed on how to interpret the Torah, there was still a strong commitment to its traditions and the God described within. Likewise, there is a high degree of social differentiation within Palestinian society. On the one hand, the priests and high priestly family would have been held to a higher standard according to the Levitical stipulations. With regard to the temple and the society, there was literally a hierarchy, a rule of the priests, in first century Palestinian society. So, in Palestine, we find a high degree of grid, a stratification and concentration of power in a few high priestly families, guaranteed by commonly held beliefs about the central role of the Torah in everyday life, high group. Likewise, as part of the wider Roman world, first century Palestine also participated in its highly differentiated status system. The Roman governor and the Herodian client kings were among the political elite of the broader Roman society, guaranteed in part through the maintenance of a Roman garrison in the temple and Roman occupation in other parts of the land, but also through the astute manipulation of the Jewish religious elites.

Enclavists, Isolates, and Jesus' Ministry

Because high group/high grid societies employ high levels of groupthink to discriminate among social groups, they often create subcultures of those who form enclaves; and those enclaves are isolated, cast out, or prevented from participating in society.

Sometimes, such enclaves develop through disagreement and choice. The Essenes, for example, vehemently disagreed with the laxity of the Pharisees' interpretation of purity law. They also became so disgusted with how the Sadducees and other priests in the temple were practicing the Torah, especially disagreeing on issues of calendar and ritual purity, that they left Jerusalem altogether and set up their own enclaves. Out in the Judean wilderness, far away from the temple and its apparatus, they could practice purity rituals according to their own strict interpretation of Leviticus. Likewise, there they could follow the teachings of the leader, the Teacher of Righteousness, and await the end-time cataclysm that had been revealed to them through their special and unique reading of the prophets. Their insistence on following their interpretation demonstrates the high degree of commitment various groups had about the importance of following the Torah and prophets in everyday life. Still their insistence that their interpretation was correct, while all others were wrong, led them to form their own enclave. Others, however, simply could not live up to the expectations of first century Palestinian Jewish purity law, no matter what they did. Those with skin diseases, epilepsy, the blind, the lame, the deaf, and various bodily malformations, those with various kinds of bodily emissions, prostitutes (because they came into contact with emissions), and Gentiles *de facto* could not participate in purity rituals, and hence were more or less excluded from much of the social, religious, and economic functions of first century Palestinian society. These folks make up a large group of isolates and, in many cases, literally untouchables in Israel's high group/high grid society.

The historical Jesus enters this high group and high grid society preaching a message of a coming Kingdom of God in which there will be an eschatological leveling, or even reversal, of the social hierarchy and a prophetic commitment to egalitarianism. When his opponents charge that "Jesus is a glutton and drunkard and a friend of sinners and tax collectors," they are charging him with associating with the outcasts, the social isolates who neither fit into the hierarchy, nor—because of their perceived impurity—cannot participate in the purity rituals and forms of worship that undergird the system of beliefs indicative of the society's social cohesion. What is astonishing is that Jesus not only repeats his opponents' claim, but seems to adopt it as a badge of honor. It is precisely this odd collection of misfits and outcasts that his movement seeks to encompass under its banner of the coming kingdom of God. Jesus gathers the sinners, the drunkards, the tax collectors, those who were deemed perpetually ritually impure such as the blind, the lame, the prostitutes, and others who were regarded as impure. He sees that, for these people, the message of the coming Kingdom of God is cause for celebration. The prophets before him have proclaimed that God's covenant is to be restored with the people of Israel. Because of this covenant renewal, Jesus invokes celebration. Jesus' practices of commensality therefore extend far beyond sharing hospitality. By sharing meals with sinners and tax collectors, Jesus was engaging in political and prophetic theater. Gluttonous and drunken meals symbolize the eschatological celebration of covenant renewal. Whether or not he actually engaged in gluttony or drunkenness is not the point. By embracing the perception, Jesus is insisting that God's covenant renewal is about to take place—and not with the elite! In God's coming kingdom, friendship will be practiced now with those who have been shunned and shut out by systems of power and privilege.

Jesus' Friendship, Fragmentation, and the (Non-)Utility of Virtue Ethics

Following MacIntyre, some postmodern Christians have taken to characterizing the world we live in as fragmented, in part as a failure of the enlightenment project to provide individuals and communities with coherent traditions that bind us to one another, in part because of the development of varying theological and ethical models that compete with the more traditional models of moral theology.[8] Virtue ethics and the emphasis upon the church's

8. MacIntyre, *After Virtue*.

49

narratives and traditions have enormous appeal to disconnected and fragmented individuals who often find themselves struggling alone to find a coherent mode and model of community in a world of multiple and contrasting values.[9] The question is whether this model, with its great indebtedness to the Aristotelian framework, faithfully captures Jesus' message and its significance to his audience. The champions of tradition and moral virtue of Jesus' day claimed not only that he was a friend to sinners and tax collectors, but that he himself was a drunkard and glutton. Moral theology is great if you are on the inside of the tradition. Jesus, in contrast, freely aligned himself with the outcasts and excluded of his day. For the excluded, strict adherence to a commonly agreed upon set of traditions and values was the very thing that shut them out of the practices of ritual purity that dominated the society of first century Palestine. As we discussed above, Jesus' friendship practice turned Aristotle's notion of friendship upside down. Instead of a friendship that assumed "sharing all things in common" among wealthy elite males, in the Greco-Roman setting, Jesus' friendships would have been viewed as transgressing status and moral boundaries. While one can reasonably argue, as MacIntyre and his followers do, that our lives and communities are indeed deeply fragmented, what we see in Jesus' practice is not a return to the traditions of Israel, or to an embrace of Aristotelian virtue ethics. While some may find it romantic and comforting to return to tradition and moral theology in a period of upheaval and fragmentation, one must not lose sight of the reality that moral theology developed in the high group/high grid society of medieval Europe. Buying into virtue ethics means owning the baggage of group think and exclusionary hierarchy that comes with it. Jesus' practice, instead, delved even more deeply into the experience of social and individual fragmentation. Jesus embraced in friendship those who had no hope in participating in the traditions and ethical requirements of the vast majority of other groups within first century Judaism.

9. One could cite any number of his works and those of his students, but a good starting place for this point of view can be found in Hauerwas, *Peaceable Kingdom*.

Jesus was friends with those who could offer nothing in return, the moral and ritual failures, the ones overlooked, eschewed, and scorned by tradition.

Jesus, Friendship, and Fragmentation in Contemporary Society

I believe that applying Jesus' friendship ethos to the contemporary experience of fragmentation of our social lives, especially in the social media realm, has the potential to yield fruit for the contemporary church. Social scientists have only recently begun to explore how new technologies such as computers, smart phones, and social media are changing the way we live and interact with one another. They describe a triple revolution in information technology, mobility, and social awareness that has occurred in recent years, the ramifications of which we are only now becoming aware.[10]

Information Revolution

The first is an *information revolution* brought about by the internet and connected devices. Anyone of us, by connecting to the internet in a myriad of ways, can access more information than has ever been available to any single human being just twenty years ago. Internet services have made that ubiquity of knowledge easier to access. Whereas ten years ago I might have been able to listen to my music collection on an iPod that I could carry around with me, now with a subscription service, I have instant access to over 35 million songs. That's mind boggling! To illustrate the ease of access and ubiquity of information, the rest of this chapter will rely upon information accessed almost instantaneously online.

As of this writing, Google estimates that there are approximately 125 million books that have been published in the course of

10. See discussion in Rainie and Wellman, *Networked*, chapter 1, subtitle "Triple Revolutions Impact…"

human civilization. As of October 2015, Google claims that about 25 million of those have been scanned, and so are potentially available in one electronic format or another.[11] The Library of Congress has about 167 million items.[12] Right now, via smartphone, anyone can explore the library catalogs of the Library of Congress, British Library, or other large library, and within minutes find almost any book in the world, as long as they have an internet connection. One can be a scholar, therefore, in rural Misenheimer, North Carolina, where my college is located. Through an internet connection and interlibrary loan, one can order and receive practically any printed book within a couple of days. Indeed, with an e-reader and a credit card, a scholar can have instantaneous access to likely over a million titles.[13] No scholar in the history of humanity, with all their travels from library to library, has had access to as much information as we have now instantaneously in our pockets!

Mobility Revolution

In addition to the information revolution, humanity is undergoing a *mobility revolution*. Isochronic travel maps demonstrate that in 2016, from London, it took under a day to travel to any destination in Europe, North America, most of South America, Asia, and the more populated portions of Africa and Australia.[14] It is estimated that there are over seven billion people in the world. This means that within twenty four hours, most people reading

11. https://www.google.com/search?q=how+many+books+have+been+sc anned&oq=how+many+books+have+been+scanned&aqs=chrome..69i57j0.6 230j0j7&sourceid=chrome&ie=UTF-8. Accessed March 15, 2018.

12. "Fascinating Facts," Library of Congress, https://www.loc.gov/about/ fascinating-facts/.

13. These are only estimates based upon Google searches. Amazon and other publishing companies guard this information closely.

14. https://www.google.com/search?biw=1600&bih=794&tbm=isch&sa= 1&ei=1KaqWuyVMcPi_Aa5vZWYCQ&q=isochronic+distances+map+2016 &oq=isochronic+distances+map+2016&gs_l=psy-ab.3...7920.10244.0.10368 .5.5.0.0.0.0.117.432.3j2.5.0....0...1c.1.64.psy-ab..0.1.104...0i30k1.0.3z1ILJF4cZ E#imgrc=gVuBXYL9fG7_lM:.

this book—depending on their starting place—could travel and physically touch almost anyone, anywhere in the world. There are approximately 6.8 billion cell phone subscriptions in the world. And while in some rich countries, folks might have more than one cell phone, even in the poorest countries, penetration rates for cell phone subscriptions are up to around 90 percent of the population. Now, as opposed to any time in human history, we can theoretically talk to almost any other human voice instantaneously.[15]

Social Awareness Revolution

In addition to the information and mobility revolutions, we also have a *social awareness revolution* with which we are just now beginning to reckon. Social scientists describe this revolution as leading to a new way of relating to others called *networked individualism*.[16] In terms of the ways that we relate to one another, time and distance no longer matter as much. With the possibilities provided by information ubiquity and newfound mobility, our communities are no longer as highly centralized and locally focused anymore. Depending on your interest, you can connect virtually with any community online. Recently on a beautiful fall day while I was working on a draft of this chapter, I was multitasking and smoking ribs in my backyard smoker. Of course, I posted the pictures of the ribs on Facebook so I could share that moment with my friends all over the world. When I got stuck at one point or another in the writing process, of course I was able to distract myself by surfing YouTube. There I found dozens of videos from people who are crazy about smoking and barbecuing meats, whether they're in Texas, Alabama, Virginia, or somewhere else. Within minutes, I had likes on my Facebook post and had visited videos from people all across the United States.

As this example indicates, our local communities may no longer be as important to us, as we make connections with people

15. Fernholz, "More People."
16. Rainie and Wellman, *Networked*, chapter 1, "Networked Individualism."

all over the world who share our interests, viewpoints, and ideas. We can express and invest ourselves in our individualized interests now more than ever. At the same time, through social media we are highly networked and connected. Instead of six degrees of separation, a February 2016 article calculated 3.46 degrees of separation between ourselves and any other person on Facebook in the US, with an average of slightly above that for connections globally.[17] This means that the friends of your friends on Facebook have, in turn, a network of friends that includes every individual among Facebook's two billion users in the world. Of course, one should use caution in drawing too many conclusions from this. Social media show individual users' messages and posts not through random chance, but because algorithms are constantly assessing and sorting users based upon interests, as determined by what we view, click on, read, how we shop, where we live, our age, ethnicity, income level, and so forth. Several years ago, I created an Instagram account for my Rottweiler. "We" are now connected to Rottweilers and their owners on five continents. Because I often post my amateur astronomy pics and click on pics of other amateur astronomers through this account, my dog and I now have amateur astronomer "friends" in North America, Europe, and Asia. Of course, all this social media activity brings to my account a fair share of advertisements for specialized t-shirts, photography and astronomy gear, as well as various pet products. Instagram is most certainly recording every moment of attention I pay to the various pictures and links on their site, figuring out a way to market my attention to advertisers and others. In a digitally connected age, massive corporations are competing to entice, capitalize upon, and market the attention of the networked individual.[18] For the attention merchants, each of us is carrying around a treasure trove of marketing opportunities in our head. It should be no surprise to hear that political campaigns and major corporations are expending huge sums to capitalize upon this data.

17. Bhagat et al., "Three and a Half Degrees."

18. For a wonderful discussion of the development of social media, particularly in relation to the history of advertising, see Wu, *Attention Merchants*.

The Shifting of Time and Space

The final aspect of the technology revolution entails a shift in how networked individuals experience time and space. Rather than events starting at one point and ending at another and being localized in one place, events now begin earlier and echo longer, while reaching beyond local space into the social media realm. Recently I took a group of students out to a restaurant to do their final exam in one of my classes. The mode for the final exam was actually a roleplay/simulation of interactions in an early first century Pauline congregation. The students were assigned various roles and asked to prepare, based upon concepts and biblical material we had studied throughout the semester. Since I wanted the students to be relaxed, I thought that the back room of a restaurant might be an ideal place for the simulation. We made the arrangements through social media. Even though we were supposed to meet at the restaurant at 6 p.m., students began messaging me and each other via social media with little inside jokes, pictures, etc. even hours before the event began. Then, as we were together in the restaurant, students were taking pictures, messaging, etc. through various forms of social media. Soon parents, other students, friends, recent alumni, coworkers, and others were commenting about this exercise through social media. After the event, with the pictures and comments posted on Facebook, Instagram, Snapchat, and who knows where else, folks from all over the US were expressing their opinions about my students' "final exam," some praising it for its novelty, others questioning whether the exercise was rigorous enough. The social media echoes of our simulation lasted for at least a day on social media. Even our university president, who has a huge social media presence on Facebook, commented the next day on the students' novel final exam experience (thankfully, her comments were positive). The network revolution not only creates a new kind of person, the networked individual, it disrupts the networked individual's experience of time and space.

I believe that Jesus' message and practice shared similar disruptive elements as the networked revolution. There are some limited things we can learn about Jesus and the Palestinian Jesus Movement through the use of historical study. As we discussed above, Jesus was preaching to a "high group, high grid" Palestinian society. This society exhibited a high degree of social cohesion in a common commitment to Israel's purity laws and vast hierarchical differentiation between those on the top and bottom rungs of society. In addition, this society created enclaves of those who chose not to fit in (the Essenes), and isolated and excluded others who simply could not fit in (the blind, the deaf, the lame, those with certain skin diseases and emissions, Gentiles, etc.). By engaging in the ubiquitous proclamation of the Good News, Jesus disrupted his followers' experience of time with apocalyptic eschatological expectations. He also displaced their expectations of where and to whom the kingdom would come, while he reached out to the social isolates of his day. Of course, Jesus and his disciples did not have smartphones. The Jesus movement connected the socially isolated and economically marginalized individuals of his day through constant itinerancy and momentum, a hallmark of the movement that was continued as the early church spread beyond the confines of Israel to spread the news to Asia Minor, Greece, Italy, and beyond, as we see depicted in Acts and the writings of Paul.

Social Disruption and the Jesus Movement

Of course, the Jesus we encounter in the Gospels has been filtered through the *kerygma* of the early church and interpreted in light of the needs of the communities the Gospel writers were addressing. Jesus' synagogue address in Luke 4:16–30 exemplifies the radical and revolutionary way in which Jesus would have been experienced in the early church. Luke is likely writing to a largely Gentile audience, perhaps located in one or more city states around the Aegean Sea in the late first century. What is remarkable in this story is that after Jesus reads the Isaiah passage in 4:18–19, he rolls up the scroll and tells his audience that "today, this Scripture has been fulfilled in your hearing." Jesus here is making a Jubilee proclamation. Borrowing on the notion from Lev 25 and Deut 15, Jesus is proclaiming "the year of the Lord's favor," the Jubilee year that occurs every 49 years in Israel. Based upon the Sabbatical laws, particularly those in which the land is provided rest from cultivation, the Jubilee called for a blanket forgiveness of debts, the return of land to those who had lost it, and the release of bondsmen and other slaves from their obligations to their masters. Since typically only the king in the Ancient Near East could proclaim Jubilee, Jesus' pronouncement of its commencement signifies his messianic authority.[19]

What would this have meant for the Gentiles in Luke's audience? The early Christian movement experienced a sense of fervent urgency and hope in the imminent expectation of Christ's return. This sense of time coming to fulfillment would have been quite remarkable for Luke's Gentile audience, since their prior experience of time would generally have been more cyclical. Moreover, Luke targets Gentiles as the recipients of the Jubilee message. When Jesus tells his hometown audience that Elijah and Elisha were sent to the Gentiles, the widow at Zarephath (4:25) and Namaan the Syrian (4:27), he is basically signaling to them that this Jubilee message is also for those who are on the outside of their society. Jesus' proclamation of good news to the poor (4:18) is meant not just for the economically marginalized, but also for the outcasts, the broken, the sick in need of healing, and even the Gentiles. Jesus' narrative audience in his hometown does not react well to this, so much so that they drive him out of town and are prepared to throw him off the cliff (4:29). For Luke's Gentile audience, on the other hand, this would have been a welcome word. For some of them, the Good News could have meant release from captivity, as their household masters converted to this new faith, or recovery of sight, as they experience miracles in their midst, and at the very least, freedom from all kinds of oppression.

---

19. For a wonderful discussion of this and its implications for contemporary communities, see Ringe, *Jesus, Liberation*.

Jesus, the Church, and the Networked Revolution

This story about Jesus, as Luke includes it in his Gospel, addresses many of the same concerns we face in the contemporary network revolution. First, Luke's Gentile audience is being called to experience time in new and unique ways. Even though apocalyptic eschatology likely does not loom as large in the Lukan audience, the reversals of social dynamics entailed in the proclamation of good news for the poor is meant to be experienced today. Likewise, there is a universal, almost ubiquitous nature to Jesus' jubilee proclamation. His proclamation is good for the starving and impoverished Syro-Phoenician widow as well as the leprous Syrian general.

When we translate what this means for those of us who are experiencing the network revolution and the experience of networked individualism, we quickly recognize that the church is called to new forms of Jubilee ministry. In a time where mobility of persons and ubiquity of knowledge is a hallmark of our everyday experience, the church would do well to acknowledge that Jesus' Jubilee proclamation was clearly global and universal in scope, and required the kinds of mobility that we see in the story of Acts. The disciples in Acts, also empowered with the spirit of Jubilee, are being sent from Jerusalem to Judea, Samaria, and even to the ends of the earth (Acts 1:8). Furthermore, just like we too are experiencing a displacement of time in the networked age, so also Luke's audience would have experienced a shift in temporal expectation, as "today, this Scripture is fulfilled in your hearing" (4:21).

Practically what might this look like? What if our churches and worship experiences changed the way participants experienced time as well? What if the echoes of worship became a part of social media experience? What if people began posting on social media beforehand, and posted pictures, experiences, etc. on social media for days afterwards? What if church were no longer focused solely on local communities, but pulled together individuals with common interests (like social justice, art, music, etc.) who were organized in classes and bands, to use good Methodist terms, through social media? What if we understood the ubiquity of the

Gospel message in such a way that we began to reach out in friendship to the social isolates of the digital age, just as Jesus did with the social isolates of his time. Why should marginal violent groups like Al Qaeda, ISIL, the Alt-Right, and other fundamentalists be the only ones reaching out to the digital isolates? We are only beginning to realize the potential for our networked experience to form community translocally. Never before has Christianity had a platform that was more attuned to expressing shared experience and vitality as we have now. What creative and transformative ways might the church engage in new expressions of community and friendship in the age of networked individualism?

4

Friendship and Racial Reconciliation

The Good Samaritan and Mission Mississippi
(Luke 10:25–27)

WHAT'S THE MATTER WITH Mississippi? It was November 7, 2012, and President Obama was just reelected for a second term. Student protests turned ugly at the University of Mississippi. Obama campaign signs were set on fire, some 400 students assembled, shouting racial slurs and profanity.[1] Really? Racial slurs and a riot? In 2012? On February 7, 2013, 148 years after three quarters of the states had done so, state legislators in Mississippi finally ratify the Thirteenth Amendment banning slavery.[2] Yet Mississippi is certainly not the only place where the racial divide persists. The right-wing rallies in Charlottesville, Virginia, in 2017 woke the nation to the reality that racism is still a serious issue in the United States. Racism extends into the church as well. Sociological studies suggest that just 8 percent of the Christian religious institutions in America are multiracial, that is, are congregations in which no one racial group makes up more than 80 percent of the community.[3] In

1. Brown, "Anti-Obama Protest."
2. Condon, "After 148 Years."
3. See Dougherty, "How Monochromatic," 65–85.

a world where our schools, workplaces, and neighborhoods are increasingly diverse, it would seem that the church is one of the most racially divided institutions in America, and sadly that remains true decades after the great achievements of the civil rights era.

The historical and persisting racial issue is just one potent feature of the culture war that has troubled our nation over the last decades. Any neutral observer of Donald Trump's election and constant statements cannot but conclude that politicians continue to use racism and the culture war to divide the United States for their own political advantage. How the Bible might be read in a culture at war with itself is the focus of this chapter. Do texts like the so-called Good Samaritan parable of Luke 10:25–37 have relevance for the contemporary situation? How might a biblical scholar engage the text in a critical academic fashion, while still yielding relevant theological insight from the text for a culture at war with itself?

In the context of the culture wars, the call to "go and do likewise" at the conclusion of the parable can be a call for contemporary readers, culture warriors, if you will, to reconfigure our imagination about how we define what it means to be a neighbor. While many readings focus on Jesus' iconic command at the end of the parable as a call to rush to one's neighbor's assistance, the narrative is engaging the reader's imagination on multiple levels of focalization, inviting the reader to see the story from multiple characters' perspectives. Friendship, which is the theme of the story, entails both vulnerability and the willingness to assist that are counterintuitive, countercultural, and surprising. Contemporary communities that engage in this kind of counterintuitive, countercultural friendship can become beacons of solidarity in a culture at war with itself.

The Parable in its Narrative Context

The so-called parable of the Good Samaritan is embedded as a narrative illustration of what it means to love one's neighbor. The story begins with a controversial dialogue between Jesus and a teacher of the law, who stands up to test Jesus (10:26) about what he must do to inherit eternal life. Jesus retorts, asking the lawyer, "What do you read?" Ostensibly, the debate involves the meaning of the written Torah. The lawyer's answer combines the Sch'ma from Deut 6:5, "to love God," with the law from Lev 19:18 to "love your neighbor as yourself" into the double love command, a combination not unusual for the New Testament, and likely similar to what Jesus himself may have taught (10:27).[4] Jesus answers him, "Go and do this and you shall live" (10:28). However, the story does not end here. The teacher of the law, wanting to "justify" himself, asks Jesus further, and "who is my neighbor?" (πλησίον; 10:29)[5] The parable that Jesus then tells is a response to the question about the identity of one's neighbor. Jesus then tells the familiar story about a man who is going down from Jerusalem, is robbed and left for dead at the side of the road (10:30), is avoided first by a priest (10:31) and then by a Levite (10:32), until a Samaritan has compassion (10:33), bandages him and takes him to an inn and pays for his care (10:34–35). After telling the parable, Jesus then asks the lawyer which of the three was the neighbor to the man who had fallen into the hands of robbers (10:36). When the lawyer answers "the one who showed mercy," Jesus retorts, "Go and do likewise" (10:37).

Parallel Structures

In this passage we find a parallel structure between the opening controversy dialogue (10:25–28) and the section in which the

---

4. Indeed, the double love command is well attested in the other Gospels and in the epistles and is quite correctly a summary of the law that would have been familiar not only to Jesus and the Palestinian Jesus Movement in specific, but also to first century Jews in general. For a splendid discussion of the double command in the New Testament, see Furnish, *Love Command*.

5. Note that πλησίον occurs here in 10:27, 29, 30. It is also the word used or cited in the LXX Lev 19:18. Elsewhere, Luke uses other words for neighbor, including περίοικος (1:58, 65) and γείτων (14:12; 15:6, 9).

parable is embedded (10:29–37). The opening controversy starts out with:

  A.   10:25: A question from the lawyer, "what must I do?"

     B. 10:26: Followed by a question from Jesus about the content of the law, "what do you read?"

        C. 10:27: An answer by the lawyer, the double love command;

           D. 10:28: A concluding imperative from Jesus, "do this . . . and you will live."

The dialogue in which the parable is embedded follows a parallel structure:

  A'.   10:29: A question from the lawyer, "Who is my neighbor?"

     B'. 10:30–36: Followed by Jesus' telling of the parable (10:30–35) and a question from Jesus: "Which of these was a neighbor?"

        C'. 10:37: An answer from the lawyer, "The one who showed mercy."

           D'. 10:38: Concluded with another command by Jesus, "Go and do likewise!"

An analysis of this narrative structure reveals several key features. First, we observe the interrogative, almost Socratic, nature of the dialogue. In both portions of the dialogue, Jesus returns the lawyer's question with a further question. In the first part when the lawyer asks "What must I do to inherit eternal life?" Jesus answers "What do you read?" In the second part, when the lawyer asks, "Who is my neighbor?" Jesus answers with the parable and then asks the lawyer, "Who was the neighbor?"

Secondly, it is important to observe that in both C and C' the lawyer answers Jesus' questions more or less correctly. Jesus of course acknowledges that the lawyer, by summarizing the law as the double love command, is right (ὀρθῶς; 10:28). Further, the lawyer's second answer in 10:37 that the one who showed mercy to the man who was robbed was the neighbor also seems to please Jesus, because it is the basis of his second exhortation to take action. Finally, the structural analysis demonstrates that Jesus' interpretation of the law is associated with *doing*, as this is the conclusion of the D section of the passage, "*Do* this (ποίει) and you shall live" (10:28); as well as in the D' section, "Go and *do* (ποίει) likewise" (10:37).[6]

Perspective and Characterization of the Lawyer

The narrator's use of perspective reveals two inside views, each in the narrator's characterizations of the lawyer (10:25, 29).[7] Each time, the inside view reveals the intention behind the lawyer's questions. The first comes at the opening of the story (10:25). The narrator opens the story almost like a courtroom scene "and behold a certain lawyer stood up (ἀνέστη), so that he might test him by saying (ἐκπειράζων αὐτὸν λέγων) . . ." The participial phrase can best be translated as a purpose clause. The lawyer wants to test, maybe even trap, Jesus with his question about what he must do to inherit eternal life. Given that Pharisees, Sadducees, and other first century Jews had different views on eternal life, it would not matter what Jesus answered, he was bound to get in trouble, regardless of how he answered. Jesus of course eludes the trap by throwing a question back at him, "What is written in the Torah? What do you read there?" The narrator provides the second inside view precisely at the beginning of the second section of the passage as the lawyer

---

6. See also Green, *Gospel of Luke*, 425.

7. In narrative criticism, an "inside view" is when a narrator, or a character that is telling a story, provides insight into the emotions, thoughts, and motivations etc. of characters within the story. For the most part, with the possible exceptions of the "we passages" in Acts and the prologues of Luke and Acts, Luke's narrator is extradiegetic, meaning that the narrator tells the story not as a character participating in the story, but as a narrator that can provide views into the interiors of other characters. Jesus, who in this passage narrates the parable (10:30–36), functions as an intradiegetic narrator in the Lukan story. He is a participant, but also a storyteller. However, with regard to most of the parables, Jesus is extradiegetic, and hence can provide inside views as well. For more on focalization in narrative theory see Bal, *Narratology*, 142–54.

begins again trying to question Jesus, after Jesus has commanded him to do the law (10:28). The narrator states that the lawyer is "*wanting to justify* himself (ὁ δὲ θέλων δικαιῶσαι ἑαυτὸν)" by asking, "Who is my neighbor?" The lawyer's intentions are either to test Jesus, to justify himself, or both.

With these inside views, the narrator is making perfectly clear that neither of these questions are a matter of the lawyer seeking out Jesus' wisdom about the law, or even wanting to establish Jesus' point of view. In 10:25–29, almost the entirety of the narrative focus is on the lawyer. A simple content analysis reveals this. Jesus speaks thirteen words (Greek), whereas the lawyer speaks thirty-nine words, the vast majority of which (thirty-four words) are citations from Deuteronomy and Leviticus, and perhaps would have been familiar or even memorized verses among Luke's original audiences. The narrator places Scripture in the mouth of the lawyer. Moreover, Jesus acknowledges his orthodoxy! By contrasting the content of the lawyer's words with the inside views into the lawyer's corrupt desire to trap Jesus, the narrator is characterizing the lawyer as one who has a desire to affirm his point of view at the exclusion of others'. The irony is that the lawyer has actually claimed nothing wrong. He is like the troll one might find in the comments section of a friend's social media post. He claims his perspective is correct at the exclusion of all others, but fails to recognize that he has not truly offered an alternative point of view.

It is not so much the lawyer's words that are awry, but his entrenched commitment to an exclusionist point of view. For the lawyer, his "truth" outweighs the needs of the other. The narrator illustrates the irony of the lawyer's peculiar predicament starting in 10:30 through the end of the passage, as the narration shifts to Jesus' voice. Jesus' parable illustrates what the lawyer seems to be missing; even as it offers a narrative interpretation of the lawyer's own citation of Scripture in 10:27. In this sense, the parable has a kind of *haggadic* function, illustrating how Deut 6:5 and Lev 19:18 are to be acted upon in daily life. Just as the narrator offered two inside views of the lawyer (10:25, 19), Jesus' telling of the parable (10:30–35) quite literally provides an inside view of the

Samaritan. Whereas the priest and Levite went to the opposite side of the road upon seeing the robbed man (10:31–32), the Samaritan ἐσπλαγχνίσθη (33), literally translated, "ate at his inward parts." This emotional and corporal reaction, translated by the NRSV as the Samaritan's "pity," drives the Samaritan to acts of kindness and compassion. He bandages the beaten man's wounds, pours oil and wine upon them, and then takes the man to the innkeeper and pays the innkeeper to look after him (10:34–35). The Samaritan's reaction to the robbed man, of course, contrasts to the other characters, the priest and the Levite, in Jesus' parable. Moreover, his compassion and pity contrasts to what the narrator previously told us about the motivations of the lawyer, who is trying to test and best Jesus in debate.

Jesus, the narrator of the parable, shifts the focalization away from the man whose fate the reader is primarily concerned with in 10:30–33 onto the Samaritan, by providing a description of his compassion (10:33) and then of his subsequent deeds (10:34–35). When combined with Jesus' concluding exhortation "to go and do likewise" in 10:37, this shift in focalization accentuates the Samaritan's extraordinary moral exemplarity for the reader of this passage. This shift in focalization also draws the reader's attention away from the lawyer's original question. Note that the lawyer actually had asked, borrowing the terminology from Lev 19:18, "Who is *my* πλησίον? Who is *my* neighbor?" (10:29). The lawyer is *not* asking to whom he can be a neighbor. The lawyer is not asking whom he needs to go help. He is actually asking who can be *his* neighbor. Cast in this manner, the lawyer is actually asking whom he should love, potentially in return for neighborly compassion shown to him. In other words, if the Samaritan was the neighbor to the man who has been robbed, he too potentially would be the kind of neighbor that the lawyer is hoping to identify.

From the lawyer's perspective, therefore, Jesus' parable functions as a kind of "neighbor quest."[8] It is true that the narrative

8. Tannehill, who claims that Luke uses the quest story as a kind of pronouncement story more typically than the other Gospels, does not categorize 10:25–37 as a quest story. Still, the elements that Tannehill describe line up: someone approaches Jesus with something important to human well being; we

audience, possibly influenced by the narrator's negative character-
ization of the lawyer earlier, will likely see the lawyer figured in the
characters of the priest and Levite who fail to act with compassion. The irony of the parable is that the lawyer's own question
equates him with the one who has been beaten and left by the side
of the road. Again, his question in 10:29 was not, "What does it
mean for me to be a neighbor to someone in need?" but simply,
"Who is my neighbor?" Indeed, Jesus returns to this question at
the end of this parable, "Which of these three seems to you to have
been a neighbor *to the one who fell among thieves?*" (10:36).[9] Jesus'
question here revisits the lawyer's ignorance about his neighbor's
identity (10:29) and equates it to the predicament of a man who
has been left for dead and is waiting for someone to show him
mercy (10:30). The passage, therefore, does not necessarily contrast the lawyer's pride with the Samaritan's compassion. I would
challenge readers, instead, to *equate* the lawyer's pride, resistance,
and entrenched commitment to excluding others with the brokenness and vulnerability of a nameless man left for dead on the side
of the road. This man is not helped by one of his kinsmen or by
someone who shares equal trust in the hierarchies of religious institutions—as the lawyer would expect. Instead, this man is helped
by a socioreligious outcast whose presence in the vicinity of Jerusalem and the temple establishment would have been all the more
confounding.[10]

---

are shown whether the person was successful or unsuccessful; the conversation in the scene will highlight the person's progress in the quest. Tannehill,
Narrative Unity, 1:111.

9. Jesus does not tell the story in order to answer the lawyer's original question about what one must do to earn eternal life, as Green suggests (*Gospel of
Luke*, 425). Jesus, in Socratic fashion, has already led the lawyer to reframe that
original question. The concern shifts away from earning salvation to a focus
about identifying the meaning of friendship.

10. See Green, *Gospel of Luke*, 431.

The Passage in the Context
of Greco-Roman Friendship Norms

It may seem counterintuitive to read this passage as a text on friendship, especially since the φιλέω lexeme occurs nowhere in the text. However, the question is not so much about whether the text itself overtly uses words associated with friendship language, but whether phraseology, narrative themes, and certain philosophical conceptions might have been recognizable as such by the text's historical audience. There are five arguments for why that might be the case.

First, contrary to much popular talk from the pulpit about "*agape* love," the New Testament's preference for the ἀγαπάω lexeme to express the character of early Christian communal bonds does not exclude other kinds of usage. Indeed, the ἀγαπάω lexeme can sometimes be synonymous with φιλέω. In fact, Luke uses both lexemes interchangeably to express preference. In Luke 11:43, Jesus offers an invective against "you Pharisees, you love (ἀγαπᾶτε) the front seats in the synagogues." In Luke 20:46, Jesus berates the scribes, "who love to be greeted in the agora" (φιλούντων ἀσπασμοὺς ἐν ταῖς ἀγοραῖς). So, the use of ἀγαπάω in 10:27 does not necessarily point to "agape love," the unique bond of early Christian community. Instead, it is derived more likely from the LXX rendering of the Sh'ma. The love one might have toward one's neighbor could have easily been expressed in friendship relations as well.

Secondly, Luke places the words *friends* and *neighbors* in the same word field on multiple occasions. In the parables of the lost sheep and lost coin, the shepherd and widow call together friends (φίλους) and neighbors (γείτονας) to celebrate with them (15:6, 9). Later, in the parable of the lost son, the elder son complains because he has not been able to celebrate with his friends (15:29), while the father is holding a party with his servants and kinsmen over the return of the prodigal. Thus, for Luke, "friends" and "neighbors" describe similar kinds of joyous fictive kinship relations that are possible in the kingdom of God.[11]

Thirdly, as my previous work has demonstrated, Luke's understanding of friendship is highlighted in the narrative summaries of Acts 2:42–47 and 4:32–35. There, the typical friendship phrase, "sharing all things in common," is used in the context of believers. However, this typical idiom would have clearly been heard by a Greco-Roman audience as referring to friendship. Since the function of narrative summary is to draw the reader's attention to significant themes within the narrative, it is not a stretch to see Luke 10:25–37 as a narrative contributing to the distinctive Lukan understanding of friendship exemplified in the narrative summaries.[12]

In *De Vita Pythagorica*, Iamlichus tells the story of extraordinary friendship among Pythagoreans (33.237–38).[13] To illustrate the saying that "good men, even dwelling in earth's farthest parts, are friends to one another even before they become acquainted and conversant," he tells a story not entirely dissimilar from the Good Samaritan parable. The story involves a traveler who is going down a lonely and long road who succumbs to a "persistent and grievous" illness. When he comes to an inn, an innkeeper takes him in and provides everything for him, sparing no expense. Before the man dies, he writes a symbol on a writing tablet and orders the innkeeper to hang the tablet at the door of the inn, if he should die. The story concludes with a fellow traveler who recognizes the Pythagorean's sign and more than compensates the innkeeper for his expenses. While the story diverges somewhat from that of the Good Samaritan, the narrative form of a traveler in distress receiving unexpected and extraordinary assistance from a stranger would have been cue enough for a Greco-Roman audience to recognize this as a parable about friendship.

11. See footnote above on πλησίον. See also Hume, *Early Christian Community*, 109.

12. See Hume, *Early Christian Community*, 80–87.

13. For critical text and translation of this work, see Dillon and Hershbell, *Iamblichus*.

Finally, the formulation of Lev 19:18, the so-called golden rule, would have been familiar to those conversant in the Greco-Roman discussion of friendship. The command that you shall love your neighbor as one's self (ἀγαπήσεις τὸν πλησίον σου ὡς σεαυτόν) does not differ all that much from Aristotle's teaching that the friend is another self (ἔστι γὰρ ὁ φίλος ἄλλος αὐτός, 1166a.30–34). The common friendship idiom of "friends having all things in common" and "have a single soul" agree with his understanding of self-regard as the source of friendship (1168b.7–9); since one cannot have more in common with anyone else but with one's self, and only with one's self is a person truly of "one soul" (1168b1–12).

Combined, all of these arguments point to Luke 10:25–37 being heard by Luke's historical Greco-Roman audience as a teaching about friendship. For the lawyer, the parable Jesus tells may be a kind of interrogative "neighbor quest"; for the historical audience, it sounds themes familiar from the Greco-Roman discourse on friendship.

Luke 10:25–37, therefore, is not exclusively about the moral exemplarity of the Samaritan. In fact, a close narrative reading of the story shows that is far more of a *midrash*, an interrogative searching about who one's neighbor is, about what it means to give up one's trust in socioreligious distinctions, to become vulnerable, and to experience compassion from a surprising stranger. From a representational standpoint, the narrative is again far less about the moral exemplarity of the Samaritan and more about the surprising meaning of human frailty and friendship in God's kingdom, even and especially when one comes to Jesus with a hardened and exclusionary point of view.

Mission Mississippi and a Theology of Friendship

So what does my reading of the Good Samaritan passage have to do with contemporary issues such as racism? A good place to start answering that question might be to engage in discussion of Peter Slade's monograph, *Open Friendship in a Closed Society: Mission*

Mississippi and a Theology of Friendship. Mission Mississippi is an evangelical nonprofit organization formed in the 1990s that seeks to overcome the deep racial divide between African American and white Christians by fostering individual friendships, church partnerships, and economic development opportunities. Slade's work describes the background, development, and practices of Mission Mississippi. He then places that work in discussion with such theologians as Jürgen Moltmann and Miroslav Volf to develop a "lived theology" of friendship.

A statewide ecumenical racial reconciliation effort, Mission Mississippi formed in order to "change Mississippi one relationship at a time" by building and creating interracial friendships.[14] An alliance of white businessmen, African American ministers, and community development efforts, the organization began in 1992 with the aim of holding large scale events for big-name speakers, black and white, from evangelical organizations. The book focuses on the development of Mission Mississippi, evolving from an organization that planned large-scale events to a grassroots organization that developed networks of interracial church partnerships, and encouraged small-scale, local interracial prayer breakfasts.[15] Slade asks whether Mission Mississippi, with its individualistic perspective on building friendships across racial lines, is up to the task of addressing serious systemic social justice problems. Emerson and Smith, for example, in their sociological analysis of evangelical religion and the racial divide in US, claim that this individualistic perspective on religion—and the white evangelicals who adhere to it—do more to perpetuate racism than to reform US society.[16] Slade, through his analysis of Mission Mississippi and an engagement with the contemporary theologians Jürgen Moltmann and Miroslav Volf, develops a friendship theology that purports to do just that: address the systemic issues of justice while maintaining a focus on friendships among individuals. The question I am asking

14. Slade, *Open Friendship*, 1.

15. Slade traces this history in chapter 3 of this book.

16. As quoted in Slade, *Open Friendship*, 4.

here is how my reading of the Good Samaritan parable might be placed into this conversation.

Slade provides a good starting place for this conversation in his discussion of Volf's concept of the "embrace." The concept of the embrace addresses the deficiencies of the two extremes of existing practices of reconciliation within the church. On one extreme, forgiveness and reconciliation that is practiced *outside* or prior to justice—often characterized by ignoring past and ongoing injustices in order to instill superficial relationships—is flaccid and compromised. Receiving easy forgiveness, the oppressor continues in a pattern of systemic sin and abuse; while the needs of the oppressed for true justice go ignored. This is "cheap" reconciliation. In the other extreme, strict reconciliation—that occurs only after all wrongs have been addressed and righted—proves problematic in its application. This kind of reconciliation is simply often not realistic or achievable. The single-minded pursuit of justice, without a realistic hope for achieved reconciliation, quickly morphs into acts of vengeance that are destructive to those who were both formerly oppressors and oppressed.[17] When we shun "cheap reconciliation," but find ourselves incapable of the requirements of "strict reconciliation," we remain in a state of apathy and helplessness. This only perpetuates the conflict.

Volf's concept of the "embrace" seeks to overcome this impasse. He offers the concept of the "*will* to embrace," which does not demand a specific kind of moral performance from one's enemy. Instead, the "*will* to embrace" represents an attitude, grounded in Christian experience, that enables Christians to unconditionally embrace our enemies. Once we do so, our eyes—and hopefully the eyes of our enemies—open to see things from the other's perspective. Full and true reconciliation requires this expansion of vision, the ultimate consummation of which will be eschatological. The "will to embrace," therefore, initiates and accompanies the process of reconciliation, which in Christian theology will ultimately only be completed in the Kingdom of God. When through the "will to embrace," I begin to hear and see the other's truth and claims to

17. Slade, *Open Friendship*, 126.

justice, "the self of the other matters more than my truth."[18] Thus, Volf's concept of "the embrace requires a reflexive truth telling that he calls 'double vision.'"[19]

Slade claims that this "double vision" of Volf's unconditional embrace is precisely what is occurring in the small twice-weekly interracial prayer meetings held by Mission Mississippi. He describes two such prayer meetings in his book, one held in a mostly white upscale private suburban high school in northeast Jackson, Mississippi, and another in a Missionary Baptist church in a rundown drug-infested neighborhood in Jackson. In both meetings, a group of about twenty people gather, mostly evenly distributed between African Americans and whites. After a brief reflection, held by one of the leaders of the hosting congregations, the meeting breaks up into small groups of three or four. Usually interracially mixed, these groups pray over one another's prayer concerns, as well as the printed prayer concerns that have been put together by the staff of Mission Mississippi. In reflecting on the practice of interracial, intercessory prayer, Slade argues that this is the practice of "double-vision" called for in Volf's concept of the unconditional embrace, the willingness "to hear and understand the other's truth and then seek to see themselves and their claims to justice and truth from this new perspective."[20] "The small group prayer meeting" as Slade concludes, "is the space in Modern American culture where people tell their stories to others with candor and frequency."[21] Slade describes the experience of a white Episcopalian, who had never prayed with an African American before, realizing that in the practice of intercessory prayer, he had unwittingly made himself vulnerable, sharing his needs and concerns, and then felt uplifted and bonded to his prayer partner in profound ways. Likewise, Slade describes an African American woman who felt sustained and emotional and spiritually uplifted by her white prayer partners. The practice of "double vision"

18. Slade, *Open Friendship*, 128.

19. Slade, *Open Friendship*, 128.

20. Slade, *Open Friendship*, 165.

21. Slade, *Open Friendship*, 165.

requires making oneself vulnerable by sharing one's own story, while also listening with sensitivity to the brokenness, betrayal, and sorrow of another's.

Through the work of Mission Mississippi, this kind of "double vision" of unconditional embrace is creating one friendship at a time. This network of individual friendship, likewise, has the potential to erode at the systemic confines of apathy and injustice that perpetuate the racial divide. Racial reconciliation may not occur overnight. Americans often seek instant practical and political solutions to solve deep-seated historic problems. In truth, both are needed. By registering people to vote, challenging and changing laws for racial segregation, the civil rights movement made momentous positive changes for American society. Much also remains to be done. Yet churches, friendships, and communities still remain largely divided in the American South. The work of organizations like Mission Mississippi and their friendship practices are beginning to change the culture and context, so that the process of full reconciliation can be experienced in our lifetimes.

My reading of Luke 10:25–37 eschewed the simplistic interpretation of viewing the Samaritan as a moral exemplar for the reader. Instead, in telling the parable to a lawyer who is only interested in justifying his own perspective, Jesus responds with a story that takes the lawyer on a "neighbor quest." Jesus is engaging in an imaginative and interrogative narrative searching, a *midrash* if you will, about who one's true friend is. This is an urgently needed enterprise in a culture torn by culture wars, racism, and violence. Like the lawyer, many of us know Scripture. We know the double command to love God and love our neighbors. Still, we come to Scripture with schemes and stratagems to justify our own exclusionary perspectives. In order for us to be right, the other must be wrong; even if our own words ironically justify the very perspective of the other.

What's the matter with Mississippi? Mississippi is us all. With the Trump presidency and the experience in Charlottesville, Mississippi no longer merely represents a backwater of racial tension in an otherwise enlightened nation or world. Mississippi represents the human need to justify one's own perspective at the exclusion of the other. It is the lawyer asking who his neighbor is, while trying to mask his own vulnerabilities and brokenness through his aggression and inability to perceive the other.

What we discover through the parable of the Good Samaritan is the kind of friendships that are being practiced in the twice weekly prayer breakfasts held by Mission Mississippi. The "double vision" of friendship entails articulating one's own vulnerabilities, while exercising compassion for the justice, needs, and vulnerabilities of one's enemy. Embracing one's own vulnerabilities can best be achieved if we eschew the notion that the parable presents the Samaritan as a moral exemplar who models charity toward the other. Rather, rich Americans, white Americans especially, need to see themselves in the place of the lawyer. To experience their own vulnerabilities, white Americans could learn a lot by understanding that the moral exemplar in the story is the man who has been beaten, robbed, and left on the side of the road to die. Only then will we be able to see our enemy's claim for justice, when the Samaritan, the person who is both surprising and counterintuitive to one's otherwise closed perspective, comes along tending to our vulnerabilities.

At the heart of the parable of the Good Samaritan is an embrace, so beautifully depicted in Western art (for example Van Gogh's painting), between an unexpected friend and a vulnerable stranger in need. It is this same embrace that is at the heart of Mission Mississippi's twice weekly prayer breakfasts. What's the matter with Mississippi? Mississippi is changing one friendship at a time. Our conflict-rife nation may not see true racial reconciliation until the eschatological in-gathering at the end of days; but that dream is spelled in the name of authentic friendships. Dr. King reminded his nation in 1966, "I have a dream that one day on the red hills of Georgia sons of former slaves and sons of former slave-owners will be able to sit down at the table of brotherhood. I have a dream that one day even in the state of Mississippi, a state sweltering with the heat of injustice, sweltering with the heat of oppression, will be transformed into an oasis of freedom and justice." The willingness to sit down at the "table of brotherhood," former oppressor and oppressed alike, describes the "will to embrace." Sustained by friendships borne of vulnerability—Good Samaritan friendships—deep and lasting reconciliation will be achieved only through the deeply human experience of embrace.

5

Learning to Be Friends of God

Narrative Deficiency, Moralistic Therapeutic Deism, and North American Teens (Acts 2:41–47; 4:32–35)

RECENTLY, I HAVE BEEN having curious experiences in the class-room with the mostly teenage students I teach on the undergraduate level. When I refer to Homer's *Odyssey*, or the Allegory of Plato's Cave, or even the story of Abraham and Isaac, I look out into the audience and see many, many blank stares. So I try again with contemporary examples, *Star Wars, Breaking Bad, House of Cards*—again blank stares. Perhaps I am growing old, and old fashioned. Perhaps the tastes in stories of my teenage students differs from my own. I fear though that my students may be coming of age in a North American society that is so results and assessment oriented, their family members have such busy lives, and they have been so overly programmed with sports and other activities, that they have had too little time to learn and share the rich and abiding stories that undergird our common culture.

Human beings are story telling creatures. Before being able to articulate any set of philosophical or theological guiding principles for our lives, we form our identities, relationships, and understandings of the world through the stories we hear and tell about ourselves, our family members, and our friends. Whether these stories are long, complex, and full of ambiguity, or relatively short and morally simplistic, they shape us, our values, and perhaps even the virtues we embrace or reject. Sadly, when these stories are not shared, our narrative imaginations starve. As a result, we struggle to form the kinds of complex theological and philosophical understandings that are needed for navigating a complex and multivalent world. We therefore live our lives narratively deprived, hungering to fill our need for meaning with the ever increasing supply of consumer goods, the "fruitless loops" of political and cultural conflict that keep us glued to social media, and the contrived stories that fill our TV screens, media outlets, and movie theaters. With such narrative deficiencies in our lives, is it any wonder that so many feel so lonely, even if we are surrounded by people?

Moral Therapeutic Deism

After conducting a large-scale study of teenaged youth and their beliefs, noted sociologist and professor of religion Christian Smith offers a description of their worldview, which he calls Moralistic Therapeutic Deism (MTD).[1] MTD is a kind of narratively deprived set of notions that operates parasitically in the background of a wide spectrum of denominations and faiths, colonizing and displacing their concrete creeds, beliefs, and historically distinctive traditions.[2] For the adherents of MTD, the central purpose of faith is to inculcate moral values and to offer the means of obtaining happiness. For many teens in Smith's study, the sum of their faith tradition is that it teaches them to "be nice." This is the "moral" part of Moralistic Therapuetic Deism.[3] In addition to teaching them to be basically moral people, MTD "provides therapeutic

1. Smith and Denton, *Soul Searching*, 170–71.
2. Smith and Denton, *Soul Searching*, 162–71.
3. Smith and Denton, *Soul Searching*, 163.

benefits to its adherents."[4] If the purpose of one's faith life is to "be nice," the function of religion is to make one "feel good, happy, secure, and at peace." Religion that does not offer such goods is not functioning properly. The focus of MTD, therefore, is on a God who exists, who created the world and defined morality, but "who is not particularly personally involved in one's affairs"—in short, a deistic God.[5] This is not the Trinitarian God, nor the one who spoke through the Torah or the prophets. Nor is this the one who resurrects from the dead or fills people with the transformative power of the Holy Spirit. Instead, this God of MTD functions as a kind of "Divine Butler or Cosmic Therapist," who is on call 24/7 and whose purpose is to make people feel better. But this God does not become intrusive or personally involved in the process.

MTD is not an independent creedal tradition. Again, Smith claims that it persists as a kind of interfaith parasite across a wide variety of Judeo-Christian traditions.[6] As such, it is distinctive from both secularism and civil religion, as it operates in the lives of those who are engaged actively in their worshipping communities, while providing them with some code and solace for leading their lives.[7] Smith also contends that the teenagers he sampled are likely mirroring the practices and beliefs of adult relatives. While his study focused on teens, the same trends can likely be observed in the lives of American adults as well.[8]

MTD presents a serious theological and ethical challenge to the church in North America. Not only does MTD reflect a distorted view of the God of Scripture, it reflects a disturbingly nonchalant superficiality with regard to the moral, ethical, and intellectual demands of living a life that draws deeply from the wells of the biblical narrative and Christian creedal tradition. To counter and engage MTD, I would like to offer a reading of the depictions of the early Jerusalem community in Acts 2:41–47 and 4:32–35.

4. Smith and Denton, *Soul Searching*, 163.

5. Smith and Denton, *Soul Searching*, 164–65.

6. Smith and Denton, *Soul Searching*, 166–67.

7. Smith and Denton, *Soul Searching*, 168–70.

8. Smith and Denton, *Soul Searching*, 168–70.

These depictions in Acts present a church that is sharing possessions, worshipping with one heart and mind, performing miracles, engaging in hospitality, and providing a challenging witness to the surrounding community in Judea. At the beginning of the story of the early church's growth in Judea, they offer an idyllic picture of what the Christian life might look like. Furthermore, the language of "sharing all things in common" would have been easily recognized by the Greco-Roman reader as friendship language. These depictions, therefore, offer readers a vision of friendship that is set in a complex and intriguing narrative.

Reading the Narrative Summaries in Acts

From John Chrysostom to contemporary times, interpreters have repeatedly sought in the depictions of the early church in Acts a model for the church's own practices.[9] It is my contention that these passages in Acts present a God deeply engaged with the formation of Christian community. I will show that the virtues, practices, and emotional experience of this community are inherently bound to the realization of God's purpose in an ongoing narrative that started with the Torah and prophets, is culminated in the death and resurrection of Christ, and continues after the ascension. My narrative ethical interpretation, therefore, goes beyond viewing these passages as merely exemplary for church life. Instead, I view these passages, when read in their narrative context, as having the potential to stimulate the reader's imagination to engage with the biblical narrative in creative ways. Likewise, such readers are to be engaged by the God of the biblical narrative in ways that may be surprising, disruptive, complex, creative, and ongoing.

The narrative summaries in Acts "fill the vision of the narratee" with characters who are engaging in joy-filled community that

9. In a homily on the passage, Chrysostom describes the Jerusalem community as an "angelic commonwealth" in which all things are shared in common ["Homilies on the Acts of the Apostles," in Schaff, *Select Library*, 11:47]. For a more recent example of an interpreter viewing the narrative summaries as exemplary for contemporary congregations, see Chambers, *Exemplary Life*.

is established and growing through the power and Spirit of God. The immediate narrative context of the summaries is the story of the emerging Christian community in Jerusalem after the ascension of Jesus in the beginning of Acts.

The Summaries in Their Narrative Context

The first narrative summary comes at the conclusion of the Pentecost story (2:1–47). As one would expect of a summary, it is sparse in narrative detail.[10] The repetition of the words καθ' ἡμέραν, "daily" (2:46, 47), and the preponderance of imperfect tense verbs show that the summary is describing an undetermined yet prolonged period after the Pentecost.[11] The Pentecost story highlights God's active involvement in the formation of the community through the coming of the Holy Spirit and the reactions of the surrounding crowds in Jerusalem to the disciples' new abilities (2:1–13). Peter's sermon (2:14–40) addresses these reactions and is apparently effective among some of his audience, because it results in the addition of new believers to the disciples (2:41). The summary, therefore, is a concluding description of this growing group of believers that begins to be formed on Pentecost day (2:41–47).[12] So, while the Pentecost story opens with God pouring the Holy Spirit upon the disciples (2:2–4), the summary concludes with a description of God growing the community of believers at an astonishing rate (2:41, 47).

After the first narrative summary, the narrative of Acts (2:42—4:31) continues by portraying the growing conflict between

10. This lack of detail fits one of the criteria for identifying summary discussed above. Note that Peter's monologue (2:14b–35) is a well-developed and detailed speech composed according to the ancient rhetorical guidelines for appropriateness to his character, age, and historical situation. See Tannehill, *Narrative Unity*, 2:42. Likewise, the portrayal of Peter and John healing the man begging at the temple is rich in narrative detail (3:1–10).

11. The imperfect tense verbs indicate activities that are occurring over a longer period of time. See the discussion in Chambers, *Exemplary Life*, 164–65, n. 16.

12. Wendel, *Gemeinde in Kraft*, 58.

the apostles, notably Peter and John, and the religious authorities in Jerusalem.[13] The conflict grows through a series of scenes that follow as a consequence of Peter and John healing the man lame from birth at the gate of the temple (3:1–10). After Peter's somewhat accusatory (3:12–26) speech to the astonished crowds who have run (3:11) to witness the recently performed miracle (3:1–10), the authorities quickly move to arrest and try them (4:1–22). However, because they can find nothing against them (4:13) and realizing that Peter and John have the favor of the people (4:21), the authorities release Peter and John (4:23). The second narrative summary (4:3–35) follows the community's prayer of thanksgiving for their release (4:24–31). The narrative between the first and second summaries is addressing questions about the source of the apostles' ability to heal (3:12) and the source of confidence with which they proclaim bold (4:13) truths to their narrative opponents. As the community is granted (4:31) the boldness that it requests (4:29), the ground shakes, thus demonstrating that the source of their confidence is God. This boldness in the face of resistance will continue to characterize the community's proclamation throughout Acts.[14]

By repeating certain keywords and phrases, Acts 2:41–47 and 4:32–35 draw the attention of the narrative audience to certain themes and motifs that one can find throughout Luke-Acts. A detailed analysis of how the summaries accomplish this lies beyond the scope of the present work and has been published by me in other venues. However, a study of these passages reveals that, in the presence of God, the believers are engaging in three kinds of community practices that resound broad motifs from the wider Lukan narrative. Through their teaching (2:42), testimony (4:33),

13. There are basically three elements of the conflict: 1) the apostles are viewed as a threat by the authorities (4:1–3, 7) for teaching in the temple (3:11–26); 2) the resurrection content of their teaching is problematic for the Sadducees (4:1–2); and 3) their apparent sway over the people awakens jealousy among the hierarchy (4:16–17; 5:17). These three elements are intertwined in the authorities' continued resistance to the plan of God in the narrative. See Tannehill, *Narrative Unity,* 2:59.

14. Tannehill, *Narrative Unity,* 2:61–62.

and prayers (2:46, 47), they are engaging in bold acts of proclamation. Through common meals (2:46), they are sharing hospitality with one another, even across well-established boundaries. And giving up, gathering, and distributing their properties and goods to those in need (2:44–45, 4:32, 34–35), they are engaging in the practice of sharing possessions.[15] Again, by populating the summaries with characters who engage in these kinds of practices, the narrator is placing imaginative possibilities for their own communities and lives before the eyes of the narrative audience.

Friendship Language in the Narrative Summaries

In Acts 2:44 and 4:32, the narrator depicts the believers as "sharing all things in common" and being "one heart and soul." The proverbs, "friends have all things in common" (κοινὰ τὰ φίλων) and are of "one soul" (μία φυχή), are well attested in the ethical and philosophical discourse on friendship in the Greco-Roman period, appearing in works by Plato,[16] Aristotle,[17] Plutarch,[18] Cicero,[19] Seneca,[20] Philo,[21] Diogenes Laertius,[22] Iamblichus,[23] and others.[24]

---

15. Hume, *Early Christian Community*, 78–149.

16. *Critias*, 110c; *Leges*, 739C; *Lysis*, 207C; *Phaedrus*, 279C; *Resp.*, 424A, 449C;

17. *Ethica eudemia*, 1137b, 1240b; *Eth. nic.*, 1159b; 1168b; *Magna moralia*, 2.11.49.5; *Politica*, 1263a;

18. *Amatorius*, 767D; *De amicorum multitudine*, 96f; *Cato minor* 73.4.3, (794D); *Conjugalia praecepta*, 143A; *De fraterno. amore*, 478D; 490E; *Marcellus*, 17.3.4; *Quaestionum. convivialum libri IX*, 644C; *Non posse suaviter vivi secundum Epicurum*, c. 22.4.

19. *Laeius*, 92; *De officiis*, 1.51; 1.56c.17.

20. *Epistula morales*, 48.2; *De beneficiis*, 7.4.1; 7.12.1.

21. *De vita Mosis*, 2.105.

22. *Vitae philosophorum* 4.53.8; 8.10.6; 10.11.6.

23. *De Vita Pythagorica*, 6.32.1; 19.92.21.

24. The list may include also Dio Chrsysostom (*De regno* iii, 135R); Libanius (*Epistulae*, 1209.4.3;1537.5.2); Strobaeus (*Anthologium*, 4.1.161.11); Olympiodorus (*In platonis Alcibiadem commentarii* 88.12); Theophrastus (*Fragmenta*,75.1.1); and Timaeus (*Fragmenta*, 3b,566,F.13b.2), as well as early

As we saw above in the first chapter, both Plato and Aristotle assume that their readers are familiar with these proverbs.[25] Upon hearing these maxims, ancient readers and auditors would have immediately understood them as having to do with the quality of friendship.[26]

Contemporary interpreters are generally in agreement that Luke is using the friendship idiom here.[27] Luke, however, is using these proverbs in a distinctive way in order to illustrate the quality of community among the early believers as different from ordinary conceptions of friendship. One can discern this by seeing how he alters the language of the proverb. The usual phrasing of the maxim is κοινὰ τὰ φίλων (among *friends* things are shared). Luke's narrator instead offers the description πάντες δὲ οἱ πιστεύοντες . . . εἶχον ἅπαντα κοινὰ (all the believers . . . had all things in common; 2:44). As Dupont correctly observes, it is theologically significant that Luke is not calling these characters "friends," but instead "believers."[28] By describing them as "believers," the narrator is focusing the reader's attention upon these characters' relationship with God, in addition to their relationship with one another. To use a spatial metaphor, these characters' vertical relationship with God empowers their horizontal practices with one another. In addition, this is the first time in Luke-Acts that the narrator is using the term "believers" to characterize a collection of characters. Luke describes believers who are participating in a

---

Christian writers—often following the descriptions of Acts—Cassiodorus (*De anima* 517b); Clement of Alexandria (*Protrepticus* 12.122.3.1[94P]), et al.; See also Mitchell, "Social Function," 257. Bohnenblust, "Beiträge zum Topos Peri Filias," 40–41.

25. Plato, *Respublica*, 424a; Aristotle, *Ethica nichomachea*, 1159b and 1168b.

26. Johnson, "Making Connections," 159.

27. See Dupont, "Community of Goods," 89–91. Gaventa, *Acts*, 81. Johnson, *Acts*, 59–62; Mitchell, "Social Function," 255–72; and Tannehill, *Narrative Unity*, 2:45, among others.

28. "This fact would seem to suggest that our starting point for an explanation of early Christian behavior should be the faith by which they are all joined to Christ and united to one another. This faith is the ground of their fellowship, the foundation of the *Koinonia*." See Dupont, "Community of Goods," 102.

joy-filled community, as they share meals together with joyful and generous hearts (2:46) and praise God together and experience the favor of all the people (2:47). Thus, the believers are depicted as experiencing a distinctive kind of friendship (2:44), a community that is joyfully trusting, and the fulfillment of God's promises in the narrative.

Joy in the Narratively Rich Life: Luke-Acts as a Story of Joy

This leads to a discussion of the second theme, the "joy" of the believers. Anke Inselmann's book, *Die Freude im Lukasevange-lium: Ein Beitrag zur psychologischen Exegese,* offers a thorough contribution to the study of joy in the Lukan narrative—as well as a methodological advance in the examination of emotions in biblical literature.[29] Inselmann demonstrates that joy represents a significant narrative motif in the Gospel of Luke.[30] By focusing primarily on clusters of words and representations of joy throughout the Gospel of Luke, she aptly demonstrates how the theme threads its way through the narrative. In the infancy narratives, for example, Zechariah is told by the angel "that there will be joy (χαρά) for you and rejoicing (ἀγαλλίασις) and many will rejoice (χαρήσονται) about John's birth" (Luke 1:14); Mary reports to Elisabeth that the infant in her womb leapt for joy (ἐν ἀγαλλιάσει) when she heard Elisabeth's greeting (1:44); and Mary magnifies the Lord, "my Spirit rejoices (ἠγαλλίασεν) in God my savior" (1:47). The theme of joy recurs in the three parables in Luke 15, in the Zacchaeus story of Luke 19, and comes to a climax in Luke 24:52, as the followers of Jesus return with great joy to Jerusalem after witnessing Jesus' ascension. Inselmann's work engages in narrative critical and form critical analysis of these passages.

Inselmann also summarizes and applies both ancient and modern theories about the presence and control of emotions,

---

29. Inselmann, *Freude.*

30. Inselmann, *Freude,* 1–2.

particularly joy, in the ethical life.[31] Here is another place where the work of Inselmann and others intersects with the concerns of this chapter. Whereas some contemporary North Americans are operating with a kind of Moralistic Therapeutic Deism, some in the ancient world could be described as operating with a kind of "Moralistic Therapeutic Syncretism." Martha Nussbaum, as mentioned above, has famously described the work of the Hellenistic philosophical schools as practicing a kind of "therapy of desire."[32] John Fitzgerald's collection of essays, *The Passions and Moral Progress in Greco-Roman Thought*, describes how proponents of various Hellenistic philosophical schools used emotion as a means of shaping and making progress in the moral life.[33] Inselmann's work aptly places Luke within this Greco-Roman ethical therapeutic framework. Luke's narrative, according to Inselmann, functions pedagogically, training readers in the appraisal and control of the emotional, and hence, ethical life.[34] For Luke, "ideal joy" is an extraordinary and profuse reaction to God's work that can motivate a reader to go in new and creative ways.[35]

Joy in Peter's Pentecost Speech and the Narrative Summaries

Inselmann's work in Luke is instructive as we turn to Acts and examine, first, how joy functions in Peter's Pentecost speech, and second, how joy consequently is picked up in the summary as a means of characterizing the life of the early Christian community. In Peter's interpretation of Psalm 15:8–11 LXX we see a preponderance of the emotional expressions of confidence (2:25), gladness (2:26), and joy (2:26, 28) at the heart (2:26b) of the psalmist's

31. See her discussion not only of modern psychological theory, but also that of Plato, the Stoics, and Philo, ibid., 35–133.

32. Martha Craven Nussbaum, *Therapy of Desire*.

33. John T. Fitzgerald, *Passions and Moral Progress in Greco-Roman Thought*, 1–25.

34. Inselmann, *Freude im Lukasevangelium*, 400.

35. Ibid., 401–2.

relationship with God. There can be little doubt that Peter is interpreting this psalm messianically.[36] Hence, when Peter uses the first
person in quoting the psalmist in 2:26, he is actually giving voice
to Christ's experience of God's presence in the ascension. God's
presence fills the psalmist's heart with joy (διὰ τοῦτο ηὐφράνθη
ἡ καρδία μου) and causes his tongue to be glad (ἠγαλλιάσατο ἡ
γλῶσσά μου), and thereby empowers the body of Christ to dwell
in the hope of the resurrection (ἡ σάρξ μου κατασκηνώσει ἐπ'
ἐλπίδι). Since, in Peter's Pentecost interpretation of Joel (2:17–18),
Christ is depicted as "pouring out the Spirit" (Acts 2:33) upon the
believers, the believers' engagement with one another is grounded
in a fully Trinitarian expression of indwelling.

For the narrative summary, interpreting the ethical significance of the characters' joy goes hand in hand with clarifying that
the characters are being inspired by the outpouring of the Holy
Spirit through the indwelling of God in Christ. In other words,
the distinctively Lukan friendship virtue that is being practiced
among the believers is an expression of God's life-giving, indwelling triune community, as demonstrated by Peter's messianic interpretation of Psalm 15:8–11 LXX (2:25–28).[37] God's presence,
a presence that fills the psalmist's heart with joy (διὰ τοῦτο
ηὐφράνθη ἡ καρδία μου; 2:26) and causes his tongue to be glad
(ἠγαλλιάσατο ἡ γλῶσσά μου; 2:26), empowers the body of Christ
to dwell in the hope of the resurrection (ἡ σάρξ μου κατασκηνώσει
ἐπ' ἐλπίδι; 2:26). God's presence also pervades the community
portrayed in the summary as sharing meals together at the end
of the Pentecost narrative "with joy and simplicity of heart" (ἐν
ἀγαλλιάσει καὶ ἀφελότητι καρδίας; 2:46), praising God (2:47)

36. Dupont, "Community of Goods," 105–6, 9; Juel, *Messianic Exegesis*,
104.

37. Speaking of Christian community, Moltmann also claims that "the fellowship of the Holy Spirit . . . corresponds to his fellowship with the Father and
the Son. . . . It issues from the essential inward community of the triune God,
in all the richness of its relationships; and it throws this community open for
human beings in such a way that it gathers into itself these men and women
and all other created things, so that they find eternal life." See Moltmann, *Spirit
of Life*, 219.

daily in the temple (2:46), in prayer (2:42), and sharing common property across socioeconomic and status boundaries (2:44–45).[38] In Peter's messianic interpretation, God's "face," God's perceptible presence, fills Christ with joy in the resurrection (2:28). Through their friendship practices, it is as if all the believers were singing out the words of Christ with the psalmist, "You will fill me with joy in your countenance" (2:28).

The Narrative Summaries of Acts and the North American Church

So how does this reading of the summaries address the contemporary situation of the church in North America, especially if it is permeated by Moralistic Therapeutic Deism (MTD)? This chapter began with recent findings by a sociologist of religion who has discovered the prevalence of an underlying religious expression among youth and their parents in the North American church. As it turns out, this Moralistic Therapeutic Deism may well share some features with its counterparts in the ancient world, namely the "Moralistic Therapeutic Syncretism" of the Greco-Roman philosophical schools. Just as Luke's narrative opened imaginative possibilities for early Christians navigating the philosophical and ethical assumptions of their world, might it also open imaginative and creative possibilities for contemporary Christians as well? Given the immensely diverse contexts of possible reading audiences, I do not believe that such a reading can or should provide simple answers or clear judgments on specific ethical issues. Nor should a reading of the narrative provide a specific teleological appraisal of the biblical narrative. The depictions of the early church in Acts are not a model for us. Furthermore, unlike some contemporary virtue ethicists, I would not claim that the narrative somehow helps us to reclaim certain virtues, traditions, or values with regard to character formation.

---

38. Mitchell, "Social Function," 255–72.

Instead, here and throughout this book, I am engaging in a kind of narrative ethics. As a literary method, narrative ethics assists the interpreter in unlocking the potential of the narrative to shape and evoke readers' imaginations, while describing how readers may embrace and be embraced by characters in the narrative. As a literary technique, the basic insight of narrative ethics is that real-world readers, through the very act of reading, imaginatively conceptualize the relationships among the various characters that are being configured by the narrator for the narratee, while also forming relationships with the narrator and the characters being described in the narrative. Thus, the reading of stories is inherently a relational practice. Scholars of biblical narratives, especially those of us who undertake their scholarship from a confessional perspective, have an ethical responsibility to articulate the kinds of potential relationships we see functioning within a particular text. We also have a responsibility to provide our reading communities with guidance and direction in how to embrace or be embraced by these characters.

Rediscovering God's Story

So what advice would I give? I would want North American congregations to engage the story in Scripture in such ways that the surprising, counterintuitive, and creative elements within it become imagined possibilities within the minds, lives, and communities of those who read it. My contention is that in spite of all of our information technology and our ability to travel, our networked, individualistic generation is hungering for authentic, profound, and surprising narratives. That is why, I think, we see in our contemporary media a craven desire for the most salacious and titillating stories, the kinds of stories that go viral on the various online and cable media outlets. It may even explain how someone like Donald Trump could get elected. In studying and describing the basic premises of MTD, it is simply depressing how little complexity, conflict, suspense, development, and narratival perspective they evince. An excerpt from one of the teen's interviews with Christian Smith's team demonstrates this narrative vacuum:

> Interviewer [I]: When you think of God, what image do you have of God?
>
> Teen [T]: [yawning]
>
> I: What is God like?
>
> T: Um, good. Powerful.
>
> I: Okay, anything else?
>
> T: Tall.
>
> I: Tall?
>
> T: Big.
>
> I: Do you think God is active in peoples' lives or not?
>
> T: Ah, I don't know.
>
> I: You're not sure?
>
> T: Different people have different views of him.
>
> I: What about your view?
>
> T: What do you mean?
>
> I: Do you think God is active in your life?
>
> T: In my life? Yeah.
>
> I: Yeah, hmm. Would you say you feel close to God or not really?
>
> T: Yeah, I feel close. [yawns]
>
> I: Where do you get your ideas about God?
>
> T: The Bible, my mom, church. Experience.
>
> I: What kind of experience?
>
> T: He's just done a lot of good in my life, so.
>
> I: Like, what are the examples of that?
>
> T: I don't know.
>
> I: Well, I'd love to hear. What good has God done in your life?
>
> T: I, well, I have a house, parents, I have, I have the Internet, I have a phone, I have cable.[39]

39. Smith and Denton, *Soul Searching*, 135.

So for this 14-year-old white Protestant girl from Idaho, her story with God is that he is big, tall, and powerful, and has somehow managed to give her the Internet, a cell phone, and cable TV. What would happen if, just for a moment, this young teen could step into the Lukan story world and find herself among the believers of the early Jerusalem community that are depicted in Acts 2:41–47 and 4:32–35? Maybe, instead of seeing God as a divine butler and on-call therapist, she might begin to experience a community of friends that are living into God's joy-filled, indwelling presence in surprising and counterintuitive ways. Perhaps she might discover a God whose narrative with humanity twists and turns its way through the suspenseful stories of Israel all the way back to the stories of creation. Perhaps she will learn the stories of God who is at work through Jesus' preaching and healing ministry, as well as his crucifixion and resurrection. Maybe in *Acts* she will discover a God who is present in the overwhelming successes and disheartening setbacks of the church's continuing and ongoing story. Caught up in this story, she might begin to experience the true joy of the resurrection and realize the complexity of being in relationship with this God in Christian community, all the while recognizing in her own experience and community those moments when God is filling her with joy. Seeing herself as a participant in this ongoing and exciting narrative, perhaps she'll begin to conceive of and strategize ways in which she might engage through her community in the transformed friendship practices of the early Jerusalem community: sharing possessions with those in need, offering hospitality to the strangers among us, and boldly speaking articulate words about the surprising story with God that she has received and continues to experience on a daily basis.

6

A Friend Lays Down His Life

PTSD and the Johannine Community
(John 15:13)

AT LEAST SINCE SEPTEMBER 11, 2001, if not longer, the United States has had its Janus doors opened. Whether we recognize it or not, we are in a state of perpetual war. Our soldiers are posted not only in Afghanistan, but all around the world, actively combatting real and also likely contrived terrorist threats. Meanwhile, at home, a culture war is raging between right-wing extremists and left-wing progressives, with conflict between the races at its highest since the 1960s. In many ways, the underlying fear our culture has experienced since September 11 merely stokes the fires of the culture war, draining us emotionally and damaging our interpersonal relationships. Many of us in this culture at war yearn for peace. As the Jesus of the Fourth Gospel departs from his community, he does so with repeated calls to peace (John 14:27; 16:33; 20:19, 21). Living as we do in a world at war, how are we to understand that peace? Can a renewed sense of friendship help us, in our communities, to do as the spiritual based upon Isa 2:4, and calls us to "study war no more?" Ironically, the ones who can teach us most about peace and friendship may be the veterans among us who have seen actual combat. Veterans, especially those who suffer PTSD, manage the physical and psychological stresses of having experienced real combat on a daily basis. Many of them are motivated to find peace, true and lasting peace. They also know the true value of friendship.

Valuing Veterans' Experiences

In this chapter, I will be reading portions of John's Gospel, especially those concerned with friendship, from the perspective of veterans returning from wars in Iraq and Afghanistan. My interest in this topic stems from encounters with two students. Both of these students were veterans of recent wars in Iraq or Afghanistan. Each shared traumatic stories of loss and brokenness to their classmates and myself in class. In my Bible and World class, I try to engage my students with the concept of how different reading communities might engage the biblical text in distinctive ways. For their final papers in the class, I try to encourage the students to engage a reading community in which they are interested or which they represent. As one of my veteran students and I began to explore the literature, however, we found that there was a real paucity of readings through the distinctive hermeneutical lens of veterans returning from war. As a result, my student, who had held a dying comrade in his arms, could find little academic reflection on how such experiences might impact his reading of the Bible. Another student dealing with PTSD shared an even more troubling story. She recounted how a soldier and veteran of multiple tours had returned to base after a bloody ambush and firefight in Afghanistan. On base, when he sought to work through his frayed nerves with a busy and distracted chaplain, the chaplain asked him to sit down in his office and read Matt 5:43–48 while he stepped out to take care of some other errands. While reading the antithesis in which Jesus calls on his audience to "love your enemies . . . and be perfect as your heavenly father is perfect," the soldier took out his sidearm and killed himself. While these two stories raise many questions, one thing they do illustrate is the need for rigorous academic engagement to develop an interpretive lens that reads the Bible from the perspective of veterans with PTSD.

Methodological Reflections

In John 15:13, Jesus tells his disciples, "No one has greater love than this, to lay down his life for his friends." This chapter uses a narrative ethical methodology to engage the passages in which John is using Greco-Roman friendship language from the perspective of US veterans returning from the Iraq and Afghanistan wars. As we have discussed in each of the chapters of this book, narrative ethics operates with three methodological components—narrational, representational, and hermeneutical—to discover a text's potential to shape the imaginations and evoke emotions of contemporary audiences.

Narrational ethics provides a narratological interpretation of the story, a close reading that attends to the rhetorical dynamics of the story in its narrative context. In this chapter, the narratological investigation will contextualize the phrase "no one has greater love than this, to lay down one's life for one's friends" (John 15:13) from the perspective of Jesus' role as a character in the Johannine narrative.[1] We will focus on how Jesus' sacrificial death in the Fourth Gospel is interpreted as an expression of friendship toward the disciples, those who are insiders in his community, while those who are outside remain in a state of conflict, dualistically opposed to Jesus and the work of the Father in John. While outsiders may view Christ's death as a defeat for Jesus and his followers, Christ's self-sacrificial death is interpreted for those inside the Johannine community ironically as a victory, a victory that indeed very much shapes the ethos and friendship of those inside the community.

Representational ethics attends to the philosophical/ethical framework from the culture in which the narrative came to be that might be represented in the narrative. The author of the Fourth Gospel is using "laying down one's life" language from a Greco-Roman friendship *topos*[2] found in Plato, Aristotle, Lucian,

---

1. Numerous studies have examined the use of friendship language and motif in John. See Culy, *Echoes of Friendship*; Elliott, "John 15:15"; O'Day, "Jesus as Friend"; Puthenkandathil, *Philos*; and Ringe, *Wisdom's Friends*.

2. For discussion of this *topos* and its presence in ancient Greco-Roman texts, including New Testament texts and particularly John, see the following

Seneca, Cicero, Epictetus, and even Paul.[3] Friendship in battle was expressed through acts of self-sacrifice, even unto death. Soldiers, therefore, knew the true value of friendship—a value Greco-Roman philosophers freely repeated and adapted. The Johannine narrator is using this Greco-Roman friendship language to fashion a narrative that expresses a distinctive experience of friendship for the narrative audience, that Jesus' self-sacrificial friendship will create a lasting bond for the Johannine community.

Hermeneutical ethics enables readers to be sensitive to the ethics of reading or teaching a narrative in light of contemporary sociocultural contexts and conflicts.[4] The chapter will begin with some hermeneutical reflections on the perspective of US veterans returning from war in Iraq and Afghanistan. As I engage in a reading of the text from the perspective of veterans returning from war, my thesis is that these veterans are well equipped as readers to grasp the irony of Jesus' sacrificial death in the Fourth Gospel. Grasping this irony, these veterans will find the Johannine presentation of friendship to be a word of hope. Contrary to cultural expectations of many characters within the Johanine narrative world, Jesus does not fall a casualty for his friends as part of an ongoing dualistic conflict. Quite the contrary, his death can be interpreted as a final victory.

Understanding PTSD

Many veterans, upon returning to civil society, suffer a kind of perpetual war that manifests itself through various kinds of psychosocial and physical symptoms. PTSD is classified by the DSM V as a trauma- and stessor-related disorder. The DSM V lists

---

secondary sources: Fitzgerald, *Friendship, Flattery, and Frankness*; Fitzgerald, "Christian Friendship"; Mitchell, "Greet Friends by Name"; O'Day, "Jesus as Friend."

3. Plato, *Symp* 179B, 208D; Aristotle, *Eth. Nic.* 9.8.9, Lucian, *Toxaris* 36; Cicero, *De Amicitia*, 7; Epictetus, *Diss.* 2.7.3; and Seneca, *Ep.* 9.10; Paul *Rom* 5:6–8. See also "Jesus as Friend," 149.

4. For development of this model in relation to the New Testament, see especially Hume, *Early Christian Community*.

multiple criteria for PTSD. First, someone suffering PTSD must have had some sort of exposure to death, threatened death or actual or threatened serious injury, or sexual violence. Furthermore, that person must experience some sort of intrusion symptoms, such as repetitive and intrusive memories, nightmares, flashbacks, or other kinds of involuntary stress reactions. A person suffering PTSD must also exhibit some sort of avoidance, whether of trauma-related thoughts, feelings, or external reminders (persons, places, things). PTSD results in negative alterations of cognition and mood such as amnesia, distorted self-blaming, or persistent emotions of fear, horror, anger, guilt, or blame. Those with PTSD often experience arousal and act out in a negative fashion, such as with irritable, aggressive, self-destructive, or reckless behavior, with problems in concentration, hypervigilance, etc. The symptoms for PTSD must persist for at least one month and sometimes result in various sorts of functional impairment.[5]

According to the United States National Center for Veterans Analysis and Statistics, there are currently just under twenty-one million veterans living in the United States at this time. Approximately 12 percent of veterans are African American, 6 percent Hispanic, 4 percent other races, with the rest being white. The largest percentage of living veterans served in the Vietnam era (approximately 35 percent), soon to be equaled by a growing percentage of veterans who have served in the Gulf War or in more recent conflicts in Iraq or Afghanistan.[6] A 2006 study found that approximately one in eight recently returning wounded Iraq or Afghanistan veterans screened positively for PTSD.[7] However, the national comorbidity study that was conducted between 2001 and 2003 found that approximately 30.9 percent of male veterans

5. "DSM-5 Criteria for PTSD," *PTSD: National Center of PTSD, U.S. Department of Veterans Affairs,* https://www.ptsd.va.gov/professional/treat/essentials/dsm5_ptsd.asp#one.

6. "Veteran Population Projections: FY2010 to FY2040," *Office of The Actuary, Department of Veteran Affairs* (source: "Office of the Actuary, Veteran Population Projection Model (VetPop2011) tables 1lL, 3L and 2L"), http://www.va.gov/vetdata/docs/QuickFacts/Population_quickfacts.pdf.

7. Taylor and Sherr, "When Veterans Come Home," 10.

exhibit a lifetime prevalence for PTSD, significantly higher than the 6.8 percent lifetime prevalence for the average population.[8] PTSD sometimes surfaces many years after the trauma experienced. It is likely that the numbers of veterans suffering from PTSD will increase as those who have returned from recent wars age.

PTSD can affect veterans' spirituality. In a 2005 study in which veterans were asked to write about their trauma, approximately 80 percent used both positive and negative references to religion and spirituality.[9] An example of a positive religious reference might be the belief that God delivered veterans from death. Negative references might be anger toward God. Taylor and Sherr hypothesize that combat and accompanying PTSD may have a shattering influence upon the spirituality of veterans. Whereas pre-combat veterans may have a sense of God as an omnipotent and all-loving being who provides a sense of order in the universe, veterans with PTSD have lost that surety. "Where soldiers once viewed God as the awesome and transcendent force active in the world, they may now see traumatic events as representative of the true order." According to Taylor and Sherr, studies show that a dualistic black/white, right/wrong view of spirituality may actually cause veterans with PTSD to distance themselves or even lose faith entirely.[10] They instead call for pastors and theologians to advocate for a faith that is complex, multivalent, and involves a lifelong process of transformation.[11]

Before engaging in the hermeneutical appraisal of the text from the vantage point of veterans with PTSD, let me say a few words of caution. I think it is important to express the limitations of my own experience and presuppositions. I am a scholar and ordained minister who has not himself experienced combat. My inclination is to come to the text with a positive appraisal for the veteran. However, as a scholar, rather than forcing my own reconstructive ideas upon the text, I will strive to step back and read the

---

8. Gradus, "Epidemiology of PTSD."

9. Taylor and Sherr, "When Veterans Come Home," 8.

10. Taylor and Sherr, "When Veterans Come Home," 10.

11. Taylor and Sherr, "When Veterans Come Home," 12.

text together with an imagined audience of such veterans in mind. It is not so much that I want to read the text *for* veterans with PTSD, but together *with* them.

There are several things that veterans, especially those with PTSD, bring to the text that those of us who have not experienced combat cannot. First, PTSD is a potentially lonely and socially isolating condition. Those who have not been through combat cannot possibly understand what veterans have experienced. Veterans have shared with me how they often feel dismissed when folks so quickly say "thank you for your service" without taking the time to actually ask or listen about what that service actually entailed and the kinds of experiences, suffering, or even unique gifts or insights a veteran might have because he or she has served in combat. Combat veterans with PTSD, as described above, bear a kind of ongoing war internally that few outsiders can truly understand. For the Fourth Gospel, with its clear dualism between the insiders' perspective of the Johannine community, and the outsiders who reject Christ and the community, the veterans' unique insider view of the experience of trauma may prove a useful hermeneutic. Veterans who have served in combat often speak of the special bond they feel with those beside whom they fought, a bond that often extends to others who also have served, especially those who have suffered loss. They bring, therefore, a unique insight to the text, an experience of friendship that few civilians can understand. Their sense of solidarity, their unique experience that few outsiders grasp, and their deep experience of friendship are all assets that veterans can bring to bear on understanding John's friendship language.

My hope is that by attuning to the special perspective that vets with PTSD may bring to the text, the close reading that follows will uncover insights into the narrative world of the Fourth Gospel that wouldn't ordinarily be accessible to those of us who have not experienced such trauma. It is possible that vets with PTSD will be far more closely tuned in to the multivalent irony, trauma, and victory that the author of the Fourth Gospel uses in the narrative to describe Jesus' death. It is my hope that a close reading of John

15:12–17 will be able to uncover not only these narrative themes at work, but connect them with the experience of veterans with PTSD in a way that uncovers a powerful and potentially transformative theological appraisal.

True Friends in John 15:12–17

I now turn to a narratological discussion of John 15:12–17 in its context. The narrative of John can be divided roughly in half. Everything before John 13:2 can be described as the story of Jesus' conflict with the world. John 13:2 sets up the narrative for a series of discourses whose intended audience is chiefly the Johannine community. The language of laying down one's life for one's friends occurs in these farewell discourses, chapters 14–17 (14:1—17:26) of John. The farewell discourses are meant, therefore, to be emic. They are intended for characters within the narrative who are "insiders," characters who are coming to grasp the significance of Jesus' identity with regard to the events that the narrator is telling. As John develops and employs the language of friendship, therefore, he is doing so in terms that are agreed upon and self-understood within the community.

Setting the Context

The Last Supper and foot-washing scenes in chapter 13 (13:1–38) bridge between the narrative of dualistic conflict, 1:1—12:50, and the "insider" language of the farewell discourses (14:1—17:26).[12] Prior to the Last Supper, the narrator has signaled that Jesus' performance of signs (12:37) and conflict with the Pharisees (12:42)

---

12. "While there are good reasons for accepting the majority view, which links 13.31–38 with what follows, in terms of plot development 13.31–38, like 13.21–30, are transitional. Jesus' subsequent discourse is intended exclusively for his friends. . . . In contrast to those who remain, the character of Judas functions as an anti-friend. He has enjoyed a close relationship with Jesus and yet spurns his friendship. Indeed, the betrayal by Judas would have been all the more abhorrent to the authorial audience given Greco-Roman notions of friendship." See Culy, *Echoes of Friendship*, 147.

has come to an end, with his opponents and the wider world rejecting belief in him (12:37). The Last Supper and the discourses that follow are for "his own whom he loved in the world to the end" (13:2).[13] The foot-washing scene (13:2–12) and the meal scenes that follow (13:13–38), with their repeated language of betrayal, the identification of the betrayer, and the language of denial (13:10–11, 18, 38) all effectively highlight the emic nature of the discourse that follows. When Jesus hands the piece of bread to Judas, the narrator offers an inside view, explaining that Satan enters Judas (13:27). The narrator then uses an aside to explain that the disciples did not understand why Jesus was sending Judas out (13:28). So, by 13:30, as night falls, Jesus is alone with his "true" disciples. Called "little children" in 13:33, they receive instructions from their master who is about to be glorified (13:31–32), even as they are surrounded by the darkness of the world (13:30).

The immediate narrative context of John 15:12–17 reinforces the emic perspective of the farewell discourses. The image of the vine and branches (15:1–11) that immediately precede these verses illustrates the point nicely. Jesus says to his narrative audience, "I am the vine" and "you are the branches." The narrative audience is encouraged to "remain" or "abide" in Jesus, and Jesus will "abide" in them, so that they might bear much fruit (15:4–5). In contrast, immediately following Jesus' discussion on friendship is a discussion of the world's hatred and rejection of Jesus' disciples. So again, the language on friendship in 15:12–17 is dominated by language intended to be understood and applied by characters who on a deep level resonate with the narrator's message and identity about Jesus in the Fourth Gospel. The effect of this would be that the imagined narrative reader of the story, the narratee, is taken into a discourse that is intended only for the beloved and loyal followers of Jesus. As Jesus calls the narrative audience of his discourse "friends," so too he is in some sense befriending the narratee. The narrator is hence providing the narrative reader with access to

---

13. Curiously, in John, the narrator nowhere mentions the setting for the Last Supper; nor does the narrator explicitly say that Jesus is alone with his disciples, nor even how large the group of disciples is that is with Jesus.

privileged, insider language. The reader is being let in on Jesus' emic language with his disciples, and hence being provided access to an intimate circle of friends.

Friendship Virtues in John 15:12–17

Within this emic discourse, John 15:12–17 accents three virtues for the narrative reader: insider love, knowledgeable servitude, and self-sacrificial love. By *repeating* significant themes from earlier portions of the narrative, the narrator draws attention to these virtues. Repetition is a narrative device often used by narrators to highlight the understanding and virtue of narrative readers.

In 15:12, Jesus provides a commandment (ἐντολή) to his disciples, "that you might love one another as I loved you." The word ἐντολή repeats four times in John (12:49, 40; 13:34; 15:12). Two of those times, here and at 13:34, the commandment is connected with the disciples loving one another. In fact the language of 13:34 and 15:12 are virtually identical. The disciples' current love (as expressed through a present subjunctive—that you might love) is to resemble Jesus' love in the past (as indicated by a first person aorist indicative—as I loved you). When coupled with the language of "laying down one's life" in the next verse, this aorist functions as narrative foreshadowing, likely of an event the implied reader is already expected to know (that Jesus died).[14] Through the repetition of the love command from 13:34, the narrator is underscoring that the insider-love to which Jesus is commanding his disciples will result in a community of friends that will be distinctive to the outside world; the disciples will be categorized as "my friends."

Chapter 15 also repeats the theme of servanthood from chapter 13. In 15:14, Jesus tells his disciples, "You will be my friends if you do what I command you." He continues in 15:15, "I no longer call you δούλους." The rationale is that, unlike slaves who do not know what the master is doing, the disciples know what Jesus is

---

14. In 15:12–14 the verbal form ἀγαπάω is being used interchangeably with the nominal plural of φίλος. In these verses the continuity between acts of loving and the resulting friendships cannot be missed.

doing (15:15), because he has disclosed everything that he has heard from the father. In chapter 13, the foot-washing scene, we see a similar connection between knowledge and servanthood. In both chapters we see the close proximity of the words δοῦλος, οἶδα, and ποιέω. When Simon Peter questions the legitimacy of Jesus washing his feet, Jesus answers, "What I do now, you do not yet understand, but later you will know these things" (13:7). Similarly in 13:12, Jesus asks the disciples, "Do you know what I have done to you?" While the foot-washing is an example for the disciples of social reversal between master and servant (13:15), in chapter 13 it would seem that the disciples don't yet entirely understand Jesus' actions. Hence follows the logion in 13:16, "Very truly I tell you, the servant is not greater than his master." The connection between the disciples' knowledge and actions is still conditional in chapter 13, "If you know these things, blessed are you if you do them" (13:17). Not all of the disciples will get this connection (13:18), as Jesus makes clear. Judas has not yet left the scene. In contrast, in chapter 15 the discourse is entirely emic. Jesus emphasizes that he no longer, οὐκέτι, calls his disciples servants. The promised connection between the disciples' knowing and doing posited in chapter 13 is now fulfilled. Becoming Jesus' friends means that the disciples share in both the action and the knowledge of Jesus.[15] They, like Jesus, are servants who know what their master is doing and expects of them.

Finally we turn to the friendship logion itself. In another section of this chapter, we will talk about the prominence of the concept of laying down one's life for one's friends in the Greco-Roman discourse on friendship (15:13). For the moment I want to focus on the theme as it occurs repeatedly in John. Already in 13:37–38, Peter declares to Jesus, "I will lay down my life for you," only to have Jesus question the assertion and rebuff him with a prediction of Peter's denial. With almost identical language in 10:11, Jesus calls himself the "good shepherd" who will lay down his life for his sheep. In the explanation of the story in 10:17, Jesus goes further, "because of this the father loves me, for I lay down my life, so

---

15. See also Culy, *Echoes of Friendship*, 164; Elliott, "John 15:15," 37.

that I can receive it again." In the arrest scene, Jesus willingly gives himself into the hands of the authorities (18:11) and on the cross he bows his head and hands over, παραδίδωμι, his spirit (19:30). Again, as stated above, the repetitions of this narrative theme accent knowledge and virtue that the intended reader is supposed to carry. Self-sacrificial love is the all-important virtue for those who have obtained an inside understanding of Jesus' message for the Johannine community.

Culpepper points out the narrative irony that accompanies the descriptions of Jesus' self-sacrificial death in the Fourth Gospel.[16] Borrowing on the narrative theory of Muecke and Booth, Culpepper describes a two-story phenomenon, the notion that the story is operating on two levels simultaneously, one for an inside audience that accepts the notions and perspectives of the narrator, and one for an outside audience that cannot grasp or rejects them. In one interpretation of the story, the narrative reader is let in on the secret shared by the narrator, and in the case of chapter 15, Jesus and his audience of insiders. Jesus' self-sacrificial death is effective in creating a loving community that shares in divine knowledge. However, the opponents (the Pharisees) and those who betray Jesus (Judas) don't get this story; and so they experience and would tell the story entirely differently. The opponents do not grasp the function of Jesus' self-sacrificial death. They don't understand that Jesus' giving of his life is done as an act of love, and indeed friendship. For them, it is foolishness, or at best, simply loss. However, as discussed above, the narratee is brought into the understanding that giving of one's life is a virtue that embraces communal love and divine knowledge, while also being an expression of friendship that is incomprehensible to the outsider. The astute reader therefore grasps that Jesus' sacrificial death is an act fully consistent with God's love, knowledge, and power, an act of glorification, not one of defeat or desperation; the astute reader gets the irony.

This, I think, is an opportune point to return to the hermeneutical question at hand. The *veteran with PTSD is distinctly capable*

16. Culpepper, *Anatomy*, 175–76.

of fully grasping the narrative irony of Jesus' death as depicted in the Fourth Gospel. I suspect that a substantial part of the negative experience of post-traumatic stress is that outsiders simply may not be able to share in the knowledge or understanding of what the veterans have been through. This *tragic* irony is likely complicated in multiple ways. A veteran may not want to share his or her traumatic experiences, not only for fear that such powerful experiences may be misunderstood, but also simply out of the desire not to have to relive that trauma through the very act of retelling. Furthermore, those who perhaps could relate to their trauma may be inaccessible or unable to help. Some may have died in the very events that have precipitated the veteran's trauma. Others who survived may be so equally traumatized that the veteran's experience of retelling such experiences would provide too little solace. As a reader of the Johanine text, it is possible that a veteran with PTSD could understand the irony of the text on an even deeper level than someone who has, for example, not experienced the traumatic loss of friends in battle. This description of friendship virtue, the knowledge tied to active love, which is explored in chapter 15, may have the potential to invite the veteran into friendship, friendship in a community comprised of disciples whom Jesus has chosen (15:16). The promise of the text is that such individuals will bear fruit, a lasting fruit that is borne out in communal love.

Greco-Roman Friendship in John 15:12–17

John 15:12–17 is clearly representing a distinctive aspect of the Greco-Roman ethical tradition on friendship. As we discussed above in chapter 1, for philosophers of the ancient Greco-Roman world, friendship was a vitally important ethical concept. Aristotle makes friendship the capstone virtue in his *Nichomachean Ethics.* His discussion of friendship in chapter 9 of the *Nichomachean Ethics* proves foundational for understanding many later thinkers in the Greek and Hellenistic discourse on this topic. Friendship, for Aristotle, is a virtue that the high-status Greek citizen practiced as an end in itself. For Aristotle, true friendship was grounded in love of one's self, but extended outward because humans are by nature social. Thus, friendship as an end in itself—as distinguished from friendships of pleasure or utility—could only be practiced between people of equally high status and equally high virtue—and was limited to only a handful of people in one's lifetime.

As noted above, the idiom that the "friend laid down his life for another" was widespread in Greco-Roman antiquity. For Greco-Roman antiquity, war was a primary locus for experiencing this kind of friendship, though not the only one. One would also lay down one's life for political and philosophical causes. The true friend, for these thinkers, was the one who would lay down his life for a comrade in battle or for a political ally who had fallen in disfavor. As I have argued above, what I think makes the Johannine representation of friendship distinctive is its ironic interpretation of Jesus' death. In the Greco-Roman usage, laying down one's life for a friend is an indication of one's willingness to share in agonistic defeat. In John's narrative, Jesus' death is interpreted as victory. I disagree with O'Day's assessment that what distinguishes John 15:13 was that Jesus actually "did what the philosophers only talked about—he lay down his life for his friends."[17] While Socrates's death was not necessarily sacrificial for others, one could certainly interpret it as grounded in conviction. Among others, Seneca and Cicero, who left behind significant works on friendship, died for political causes associated with what they would have interpreted as the good of the *patria*. Among the philosophers, statesmen, not to mention soldiers, of antiquity, Jesus certainly was not alone in actually laying down his life for his friends. What makes friendship different in John is that Jesus' self-sacrificial death is interpreted as victory and glory, and not as defeat.

Another distinctive to the narrative account of friendship in the Fourth Gospel is that the reader is being invited into a community that engages in and celebrates the kind of self-sacrificial love that God and Jesus show to the world. Jesus leaves his community with the command to love one another. As he lays down his life for them, they too in some respect are being engaged to

17. O'Day, "Jesus as Friend," 150.

lay down their lives for one another. This is their expression of knowing servanthood. I suspect that the veteran with PTSD may understand this verse in ways that those who have not experienced extreme trauma cannot. In some ways vets with PTSD bring an experience of friendship that mirrors that of the Scythian warrior described in Lucian:

> I have to speak of blood and war and death for friend-ship's sake. You will learn that all you have related is child's play when compared with the deeds of the Scyth-ians. After all it is natural enough. What should you do but admire these trifles? Living in the midst of peace you have no scope for the exhibition of an exalted friendship. Just as in a calm we cannot tell a good pilot from a bad; we must wait till a storm comes; then we know. We on the contrary live in a state of perpetual warfare, now in-vading, now receding, now contending for pasturage or booty. There is the true sphere of friendship and there is the reason that its ties among us are drawn so close. Friendship we hold to be the one invincible irresistible weapon. (*Toxaris*, 36)

In contrast, Jesus' friendship in the Fourth Gospel is not one experienced in a state of constant warfare. This is what makes John's representation of friendship remarkably distinctive for the veteran with PTSD, as well as deeply significant for those of us who live in a culture at perpetual war with itself. The veteran, whose experience of PTSD is a kind of warfare that he or she has internal-ized, appreciates the depth and power of the kind of peace that Je-sus is promising in John. Like the earliest Johannine audience who may themselves have been suffering from a kind of PTSD from persecution by the "outside world," they share in a deep yearning for peace. While the first twelve chapters of the Fourth Gospel can be understood as a story of dualistic conflict between Jesus and his opponents, the message for the Johannine community in the Farewell Discourses is one of peace. Jesus departs his community with repeated calls to peace (14:27; 16:33; 20:19, 21). The message of the Fourth Gospel is not that the Johannine community will abide in fear or continuous conflict, but that they will abide in peace, precisely because Jesus has overcome the opposition. "Peace I leave with you for I have conquered the world" (16:33) is the message of the Johannine Jesus.

The Johannine presentation of friendship is ironic precisely because Jesus' self-sacrificial death for his friends vanquishes opponents and binds disciples in loving community. In John, the irony of the cross is that it is a place not of defeat but of glory. Furthermore, in the Fourth Gospel, Jesus' friendship invites participation in a community that is practicing friendship virtues of love, knowing service, and self-sacrifice. This, I think, makes all the difference for vets who might want to reframe their experience in light of the Johannine narrative. Regardless of what their trauma may have been, being befriended by a community of disciples and offered an opportunity to practice peace through self-sacrificial servanthood may provide new sources of hope, courage, and coping.

7

Friendship, Disability, and the Form of a Slave

Paul's Christ Hymn and the Friendship Concepts of Jean Vanier (Phil 1:20—2:30)

ARISTOTLE POSES THAT FRIENDSHIP is only possible between equally high-status males. Friendships between kings and paupers, or between gods and mere human beings, are de facto impossible. Such relationships would not be friendships proper, because they would quickly turn into relationships in which services are exchanged for honor. We have already seen in our discussion of Jesus' own notions of friendship how he reversed this idea. Indeed, befriending the poor, the marginalized, and those who could not expect to give anything in return was a central part of his ministry. Not unlike Greco-Roman society, our society too posits a stark contrast between those perceived as powerful and powerless. In our hyper-capitalistic culture, the wealthy elite, the CEOs, bankers, and brokers are viewed as the capable, "can do" people, people who create wealth and value for others. Tradespeople, teachers, and others with skills, while sometimes appreciated, are viewed merely as pawns for the powerful to achieve their goals. The labor of those in the service industry—Uber drivers, fast food and grocery workers, etc.—is held more or less in disdain. Sadly, our culture assigns even less value to those who are viewed as intellectually and/ or physically disabled, in part because they are viewed as unable to produce anything of value to the hyper-capitalistic consumer. If one were to choose one's friends based upon their ability to reciprocate in terms of power or capital, the disabled would be near the bottom of the list.

In recent decades, a number of biblical scholars have begun to apply the insights and methods from disability studies to the reading of biblical texts.[1] A vibrant discourse has emerged that throws new light on these texts. In this chapter, I intend to engage portions of Philippians in light of questions driven by both Paul's transformation of Greco-Roman friendship and elements of this new disability studies approach. By using the narrative ethical model employed in each of the chapters of this book, I hope to get at a theological reading that is sensitive to God's preference to use brokenness, the brokenness of the cross, as a means of reconciling humanity and forming communities in which self-giving, other-oriented friendships are core. Because Paul's Christology cannot be separated from his anthropology, questions of Pauline ethics and theology go hand in hand. In the context of Philippians, we will be reading the Christ hymn, Phil 2:1–12 in the context of his friendship exhortations to the church at Philippi. Before we do so, however, let us turn to a contemporary context to illustrate how questions of disability, friendship, community, and a cruciform ethos can congeal.

Jean Vanier, the founder of L'Arche movement that establishes spiritual communities for people with disabilities and those who choose to live in community with them, recently won the 2015 Templeton prize. The L'Arche movement began in 1964 when Vanier invited two intellectually disabled men to live with him in community as friends. The movement has grown, now

---

1. A nice collection of essays on the topic can be found in Hector Avalos, Melcher, and Schipper, *This Abled Body*. For a succinct treatment of historical and methodological issues related to the application of disability studies in the Bible, see Junior and Schipper, "Disability Studies," 21–37.

encompassing 147 residential communities operating in 35 countries, and 1500 Faith and Light support groups in 82 countries.[2] Vanier's basic philosophy of friendship can be summed up as those who are mentally or physically abled realizing, recognizing, and welcoming their own vulnerabilities by being in relationship with those who are disabled. In one of his books, he tells the story of Innocente. Because he is so eloquent, I will offer an extended quote,

> In our community of Bouake (Ivory Coast)
> We welcomed "Innocente,"
> A young girl who became a source of life
> And great joy for the community.
> She had been abandoned as a child, left to die in the bush.
> She could have been bitten by a snake or killed by a wild animal
> But somebody saw her there, picked her up
> And took her to a local orphanage.
> When she arrived at the orphanage she was like a skeleton;
> She was dying.
> Innocente survived all that,
> And the orphanage later asked us to welcome her.
> She was still quite small at the time
> And we knew that she would never be able to walk or talk.
> We could never quite understand what she was thinking
> But whenever anyone came near her and called her by name,
> Her whole face would light up.
> She had an exceptional beauty.
> She was completely incapable of judging or condemning
>   anyone.
> She was too fragile and weak to judge anyone.
> But if people did not pay attention to her, she could feel hurt.
> One day while I was looking at her, I thought to myself,
> Jesus must be a bit like that:
> Neither judging nor condemning

2. "Previous Winner: Jean Vanier," Templeton Prize, http://www.templetonprize.org/previouswinners/vanier.html.

But terribly wounded if we do not come close to him.[3]

This is of course a beautifully seductive portrayal of a person with severe disabilities, to imagine that she somehow resembles Christ in that she is somehow neither judging nor condemning. Again and again in Vanier's writings we find such portrayals of people with disability, with the philosophy that the marginalized, the weak, the outsiders, the folks at the very bottom of the social pyramid are somehow a special source and connection to the divine for those of us who are more abled. In Pauline theology, one might say that the disabled are modeling cruciformity.

While I am not questioning the great good that Vanier has done, from the perspective of disability studies, I wonder whether there might be space to critically question some of his thinking. Is Vanier sentimentalizing the fate and role of disabled people in our society? Further, by lumping together multiple mental and physical disabilities into one category and then giving special status to them as nearer to the divine, might he be further proliferating a stereotype on people with disabilities that has existed since ancient times,[4] that people with disabilities are somehow channels of the divine?[5]

Methodological Considerations

These are difficult questions. When pursuing biblical readings from a disability studies perspective one must engage in dialectical interpretation. On the one hand, one must deconstruct theological notions that disabled people somehow need fixing or healing, or can be idealized as representatives of the divine. If Vanier is understood as using Christian theology to somehow idealize the plight of the disabled and put them on a theological pedestal, those notions

---

3. Vanier, *Befriending the Stranger*, 43–44.

4. One might think of Hephaistos, who had special gifts for making things, or the visually impaired seers and poets like Tiresius and Homer.

5. For further examples of disability and the divine in Greco-Roman writing, see Garland, *Eye of the Beholder*, 59–72.

need to be deconstructed. On the other hand, some theological ideas, especially those that undercut false power assumptions and dynamics asserted by our culture, can actually contribute to a healthy theological appraisal of thriving community. For example, L'Arche is appreciative of all people, regardless of their perceived ability to contribute to society and its consumer-minded instincts. So, on the other hand of the dialectic, if Vanier is seen to be asserting the value of friendship in establishing communities in which differently abled adults are all contributing members, this can be a substantial contribution. As I read Paul's understanding of friendship in Philippians, I shall be doing so with this dialectic in mind.

In biblical studies, this kind of dialectical interpretation is further complicated by the fact that the texts one is reading come from another period and culture. In this chapter, I will be viewing disability as a social construct. I agree with Rose, therefore, that the "concept of disability is shaped and defined by its economic, military, political, religious, social, and technological environment."[6] Indeed, I'm not at all certain that our modern, medically diagnosable category of physical disability would have made a whole lot of sense to the people occupying the urban centers of Paul's letters. As Kelley points out, "The classificatory scheme 'disabled'/'nondisabled' did not exist for Greeks and Romans."[7] Nonetheless, the Greeks and Romans were not lacking in terms describing various aspects of human physicality associated with physical disability. While the terms in Greek are sometimes vague, we do see language describing people as "maimed" (πηρός), "mutilated" (κολοβός), "ugliness" (αἶσχος), "weakness," and "lameness in the leg" (χωλός).[8] Other categories, such as blind, deaf, and mute, also occur with some frequency in the New Testament. In some cases, such physical manifestations may have been associated with exclusion from participation in economic or religious systems. In other cases, what might be viewed as a disability in our contemporary, highly technical and performance-oriented society

6. Rose, *Staff of Oedipus*, 3.

7. Kelley, "Deformity and Disability," 33.

8. Kelley, "Deformity and Disability," 33.

may not have been viewed this way in an agrarian based, lesser developed, but much more highly stratified society. As Rose points out in her study, "the consequences of (physical disability) varied from one individual to the next and from one situation to the next."[9] In fact, Rose claims that the status of persons who manifest conditions we would associate with physical disability were "defined and negotiated between individuals on a case-by-case basis within a community."[10] As such, our analysis of the biblical text should lead to imagining and reimaging the kinds of communities and friendships in which folks negotiated differing abilities, with the realization that certain images of and prejudices about what the human body and mind can and should look like are operating in the background, both in ancient and contemporary cultures.

I bear in my scholarship a hermeneutical responsibility to read, explore, and interpret biblical texts in ways that are liberating, and that contribute to thriving, non-discriminatory reading communities. In this chapter, I will engage Phil 1:20—2:13 with a narrative ethical method, the method I have been applying throughout this book. As a method, narrative ethics studies the biblical text from three different angles: narratological, representational, and hermeneutical.

One can discern at least two levels of narrative operating behind and within the letter. On one level, one can examine and reconstruct the story behind the letter. This might include piecing together what Paul says are his reasons for writing the letter to his audience, as well as the back story they share together. On another level, Paul portrays in his letter a meta-story about Christ's crucifixion and resurrection in the Christ hymn in 2:6–11. This meta-story, which Paul shares with his audience, provides an interpretive clue for how Paul is seeking to be in relationship to them. As such it is also part of the story Paul is telling in his letter.

Engaging representational ethics, we will explore the Greco-Roman philosophical and ethical concepts Paul is using in order to represent the back story he has with the Philippians, as well as

9. Rose, *Staff of Oedipus*, 2.

10. Rose, *Staff of Oedipus*, 3.

the kenotic/exalted movement of the meta-story he shares about Christ. It is likely that Paul is engaging in the Greco-Roman ethical discourse on friendship to describe the relationship he has with the Philippians. Further describing the story of Christ's kenosis and exaltation, Paul is using the Greco-Roman friendship trope to encourage the Philippians to emulate Christ in their relationship with Paul and with one another. It is at also at this point of the paper that we will explore the representations of physiognomy and reverse *kalokagathia* assumed by Paul in the Christ hymn. By invoking the language of slavery and deficiency in 2:7, Paul may be echoing common Greco-Roman sentiment that slaves were viewed as having physiognomic defects, with less perfect bodies than free Greek or Roman males. The correlation of such defects to the concept of the monstrous provides an opening to exploring Paul's language in light of contemporary disability studies.

The hermeneutical level of interpretation takes into account the moral and ethical responsibility of interpreters and their audiences as they engage biblical texts. As we have begun already, the hermeneutical analysis of this chapter will put Paul's narrative into discussion with a contemporary discussion of disability, particularly that of the work of Jean Vanier, the founder of the international L'Arche movement, a movement that has established intentional Christian communities of people with disabilities. The chapter will place Vanier's theological concept of friendship, particularly as it relates to the formation of communities of people of diverse abilities, in dialogue with Paul's understanding of friendship, community, and reverse *kalokagathia* in Philippians.

Philippians as Story

As with any letter, there is a backstory to Paul's letter to the Philippians. Doing a "narrative analysis" of the letter involves understanding this story. Instead of establishing the historical facts and contingencies behind the letter, my analysis will focus more on Paul as narrator-character of the letter, and how, as narrator, he is communicating to his narrative audience. If the letter functions as a proxy for his physical presence with the Philippians while he is away, Paul's voice as narrator of the letter is chiefly aimed at managing that separation. Throughout the letter, Paul speaks of his absence from them repeatedly (1:27; 2:12; 2:19–29; 4:10), but as is explicit in 1:8, the tone throughout letter expresses Paul's longing for the Philippians. Paul manages the separation and the Philippians' anxiety by sending Epaphroditus—whom the Philippians had sent to care for Paul in his imprisonment—back to them (2:25–30). Epaphroditus's role, therefore, is to cheer the Philippians, share Paul's story, as well as share the news of his own illness and recovery that he experienced during his journey to stay with Paul. By sending Epaphroditus to cheer the Philippians, and giving him the letter with his own voice in it, Paul is managing his friendship with the Philippians through a time of separation.

Paul also provides a perspective into his own sufferings and imprisonment, sufferings that have been compounded by his absence from the Philippians. Paul indicates that he is imprisoned (1:8, 13–14). Perhaps related to his imprisonment, Paul also expresses that he is currently experiencing distress (4:14), being poured out (2:17), having lost all things (3:8; 4:12), so much that his desire is to die in Christ (1:23). While he does not indicate exactly what the source for this distress is, Paul does believe the Philippians have responded by holding him in their heart (1:7), by keeping him in their prayers (1:19), by being concerned (4:10), by sharing in his distress (4:14), and by sending him a monetary gift (4:18). They also sent Epaphroditus to minister to Paul's need (2:25), and to provide services that they could not provide Paul (apparently because of their distance; 2:30). Again, apparently, either on his way or after his arrival, Epaphroditus became very ill, so ill in fact that he nearly died (2:27). In the meantime, the Philippians have heard about Epaphroditus's illness. Now, prior to the writing of the letter, news has reached Paul and Epaphroditus that the Philippians know of Epaphroditus's illness. As a result, Epaphroditus is distressed because the Philippians are worried (2:26).

Paul's claims that he and the Philippians share a great deal emotionally is intended to build friendship and community. Paul sees the Philippians sharing in the suffering and "same struggle" as he does (1:30). Further, they have "revived their concern" for Paul (4:10), so much so that they have dispatched Epaphroditus with a gift. Now that Paul has received this gift, he can proceed by praying, remembering the Philippians with joy (1:3-4), and having confidence (1:6) that the Philippians not only share with him their material possessions, as they have from the beginning of their relationship with the apostle (4:15), but also in some sense share in Paul's endeavor of confident speech about Jesus Christ (1:14, 25). What the narrator requests from his audience is an obedience (2:12) to "make my joy complete" (2:2), not only in his presence, but in spite of his absence (2:12). Such a request is accomplished in part through moral imitation of Paul and others who imitate Paul (3:17). It is culminated, however, by God being at work in the community of the Philippians, who enable them to will and work for God's good pleasure (2:13). The rhetorical goal of the story that the narrator is sharing with his narrative audience is this divinely enabled mimesis of the apostle, in both his suffering and his joy. The template for such mimesis is spelled out in the center of the letter in the Christ hymn at 2:6-11.

Friendship Language in Paul's Letter

At this point I'd like to step back from the narratological analysis to look at the representational frame of the letter. Recall that as we proceed into representational ethics, we are looking for the kinds of philosophical and ethical concepts that are built into the letter that are shared with the historical and cultural world out of which the letter arose. While some interpreters since the '80s have indicated that Paul's letter to the Philippians can be classified as a "friendship letter," it is probably more appropriate to claim that Paul is using language at various points in the letter belonging to a Greco-Roman *topos* on friendship.[11] In much of Greco-Roman moral philosophy, the point of using such a *topos* is psychagogic in

11. See Reumann, "Philippians," 105.

nature.[12] The purpose is to provide a therapy for the reader's desire, to lead the soul through a moral process with the result of a thriving heart and mind as an integral part of a thriving community.[13]

Paul uses friendship language in Philippians in three different places: at the beginning of the letter in which he repeatedly uses language associated with public and bold speech; in the middle section, starting 1:27, in which he calls for the Philippians' unity; and at the end of the letter in which he praises the Philippians for sharing possessions with him. In the opening chapter of Philippians, Paul characterizes his suffering as so severe that he is not sure whether he prefers to remain living, which he characterizes as "Christ," or to die, which he characterizes as gain (1:21). Paul's immediate suffering, his imprisonment, is directly connected to his boldness and fearlessness to proclaim the Gospel publicly (1:14, 20).[14] His emphasis on bold and public proclamation in 1:12–20, his παρρησία, is an expression of friendship, one that is taking on a public and almost political reality.[15] His boldness is making him more confident in proclaiming that Christ is Lord. As he weighs his options, he is struggling between "remaining in the flesh," which he considers would be more necessary and fruitful for the Philippians, or to depart and be with Christ, which he considers "far better" (1:23). In the end, Paul believes that, in spite of his current sufferings, remaining "in the flesh" is more necessary for the Philippians (1:24), in part because he is a moral exemplar for them of one who is being chastised for speaking publicly.

This dynamic of public speech and suffering becomes the basis for Paul's call to the Philippians to conduct themselves (πολιτεύεσθε; Phil 1:27) in a manner worthy of the Gospel of Christ. The word πολιτεύομαι occurs only here and in Acts 23:1.

---

12. For a discussion of *psychagogy* as it relates to Greco-Roman moral philosophers, see the collection of essays in Fitzgerald, *Passions and Moral Progress*.

13. See also Nussbaum, *Therapy of Desire*.

14. See also Fitzgerald, "Philippians," 155.

15. See also Fredrickson, "Παρρησια in the Pauline Epistles," 172.

From its usage in the LXX[16] the word has the sense of governing one's life in accordance with some kind of law. Paul then uses a metaphor to describe his and the Philippians' communal life as the same ἀγών, a kind of intense physical or nonphysical struggle, fight, contest, or race (1:30). In fact, he calls the Philippians to be engaged in συναθλοῦντες (1:27), a common struggle or contest. As we analyze the words to describe this struggle, we find that Paul may be using a word field that has many commonalities with the Greco-Roman *topos* on friendship, a word field that has three aspects.

The first is the idea that the Philippians are involved in a common struggle together with Paul against opposition that has the capacity to cause them fear. The *topos* in which friends are involved in common struggle on the battlefield, and even that a friend is willing to lay down his life for another was fairly widespread in Greco-Roman moral philosophy, occurring in Plato, Aristotle, Seneca, and Cicero.[17] Accordingly, the model he sets forth in the Christ hymn that follows portrays Christ as "becoming obedient to death, even death on a cross" (2:8).

The second element of the *topos* is the language of friends being "one soul," "one heart," or "one mind" that was also fairly widespread in Greco-Roman antiquity.[18] Paul advises the Philippians stand fest in one spirit (ἐν ἑνὶ πνεύματι; Phil 1:27) and to engage in their common struggle with one soul (μιᾷ ψυχῇ; 1:27). The *topos* continues through the following verses, as he exhorts or describes the Philippians to have the same struggle (τὸν αὐτὸν

16. 2 Mac 6:1; 11:25; 3 Mac 3:4; 4 Mac 2:8, 23; 4:23; 5:16.

17. See also my discussion above in the chapter on John. For the use of friendship language as it relates to laying down one's life for another see Plato, *Symp* 179B, 208D; Aristotle, *Eth. Nic.* 9.8.9, Lucian, *Toxaris* 36; Cicero, *De Amicitia*, 7; Seneca, *Ep.* 9.10.

18. See my discussion of Aristotle's notion that the friend is "another self" in part because friends are one soul, in chapter 1 above. The trope is fairly widespread and can be found in Aristotle (*Eth. nic.* 9.8.2), Plutarch (*Amic. mult.* 96F), Diogenes Laertius (5.20), and elsewhere. See also Fitzgerald, "Philippians," 144–45.

ἀγῶνα, 1:30), to have a fellowship of spirit (κοινωνία πνεύματος; 2:1), having the same mind (τὸ αὐτὸ φρονῆτε; φρονέω repeated three times; 2:2, 2:5), the same love (τὴν αὐτὴν ἀγάπην; 2:2), to be harmonious (σύμψυχοι; 2:2), and to experience compassion and sympathy (σπλάγχνα καὶ οἰκτιρμοί; 2:1).

The third element of the *topos* involves the language of self and other that is clustered in the verses three and four right before the Christ hymn. Aristotle was well known for making the claim that the friend is "another (one)self" and that one can only be best friends to one's self, because one is only "one soul" with one's self (*Eth. nic.* 9.8.2). At least in the Aristotelian conception, self-regard is the foundation for proper friendship. Here Paul describes a somewhat different basis for community. Paul cautions the Philippians to do nothing out of ambition or empty conceit, "but in humility (τῇ ταπεινοφροσύνῃ) to consider others as being in a higher status (ὑπερέχοντας) than one's self" (2:3). Rather than self-interest being the starting point for friendship, Paul tells the Philippians that they each ought "not to scope out the goods that belong to themselves, but those that belong to others" (μὴ τὰ ἑαυτῶν ἕκαστος σκοποῦντες ἀλλὰ [καὶ] τὰ ἑτέρων ἕκαστοι; 2:4).

By using these elements for the friendship *topos*, what Paul is describing is a community, a friendship that has the "same mind" and is of "one soul." This community is based upon each individual humbling oneself and placing others in a higher status, while prioritizing the others' goods and needs above one's own. It is friendship based not upon realistic expectation of reciprocity, but upon common self-sacrifice, the kind of self-sacrifice in which friends are willing to lay down their lives for others, like on the battlefield. As Paul moves toward the metanarrative of Christ's self-sacrificial death and divine exaltation, we should note that he is emphasizing the one part of the friendship trope, the willingness to die for another, over the part of the trope that valued the self's virtuous attainment of the good as the basis for friendship.

Kalokagathia, the Slave, and the Cross in Philippians and Greco-Roman Thought

Paul follows these exhortations to community with the moral paradigm of Christ's sacrifice on the cross in Phil 2:6–11. Paul offers a story of Christ relinquishing equality with God to take on the form of a slave, a human being. This results in his self-sacrificial death on the cross, and culminates in his exaltation by God above all of living creation as the Lord over all. Paul instructs the Philippians to have the "same mind" as Christ Jesus, who, although he was in "divine form did not consider himself to be equal to God, but emptied himself and took on the form of the slave." We can highlight two key words in the passage. First is the word μορφή, a word that not only means form, but also outward appearance in the Greek. The second is the word δοῦλος, which is the word Paul associates with Christ here. It is also a word Paul associates with his own ministry as an identifier in the prescript of this letter and in the letter to the Romans (Phil 1:1; Rom 1:1). If Paul considers himself and Christ as δοῦλοι, what does this mean for an interpretation from the perspective of disability studies? As we saw in our discussion above, Greco-Roman authors had numerous words associated with the physical characteristics often associated with various disabilities today. In ancient physiognomy, the slave was often considered the bearer of physical traits antithetical to the perfect Greek or perfect Roman. If Christ takes on the "form of the slave" (2:7), we can assume that he too is taking on such physical characteristics.

In Greco-Roman culture there is considerable literary evidence of a certain normativity regarding the ideal form of the human being. Aristotle considers the human male to be "the absolute standard of physical perfection" in the animal world (*Gen. an.* 4.767b, 7f).[19] Other animal life is considered to be deviant from the standard, perhaps even monstrous. The association of good or bad character with outward appearances becomes a preoccupation among the ancients. While one can find traces in literature

19. See also Garland, *Eye of the Beholder*, 1.

throughout the period, an entire genre of texts is devoted to the pseudo-science of classifying physical characteristics and associating them with inward character, starting with an anonymous third century BCE (pseudo)-Aristotelian treatise called the *Physiognomonika*.[20] The author associates certain physical characteristics, such as movements, shapes, color, facial expressions, hair, smoothness/roughness of skin, etc. with various conditions of one's inward character. Analogies are then made to the animal kingdom to determine how such characteristics might be reflective in human character. For example, since deer, which have soft hair, are timid around such predators as lions and wild boars, which have rough hair, humans who have soft hair are considered cowardly, while those with rough hair have courage.[21] Whether in such physiognomic literature or in the cultural assumptions and literature of the day, the resulting notion among the Greeks and Romans is that of *kalokagathia,* wherein that which is beautiful, *kalos,* becomes associated with the good, *agathos.* That which is considered bad, *kakos,* is also ugly.

The resulting picture of *kalokagathia,* as it turns out, is very Greek-centered, with a genetic homogeneity reflecting traits of the Greeks: "wavy hair, dark eyes, and tanned colour skin" are associated with bravery, whereas people with eyes/hair/skin that are too dark or too light are thought to be morally defective. Since slaves were generally associated with other ethnic groups or non-Greek nations, stereotypical depictions and representations of slaves' physical characteristics in literature also go hand-in-hand with character defects such as cowardice, weakness, and roguishness.[22] However, it is not until the Roman period that the "form of the slave" becomes associated not only with negative aspects, both physically and in character, but also with deformity, resulting in a kind of teratology of slaves. Because deformed slaves appear so frequently in Latin literature, Garland concludes that "no fashionable household was complete without a generous sprinkling of

20. Garland, *Eye of the Beholder,* 88.
21. Garland, *Eye of the Beholder,* 89–90.
22. Wrenhaven, *Reconstructing the Slave,* 46.

dwarfs, mutes, cretins, eunuchs, and hunchbacks, whose principal duty appears to have been to undergo degrading and painful humiliation in order to provide amusement at dinner parties and on other festive occasions."[23] He cites example after example of slaves who serve this purpose in the writings of Martial, Pliny, and others. Quintilian relates that Romans were prepared to pay more for deformed slaves than those who were physically perfect.[24] In fact, according to Plutarch, a monster market existed in Rome, where wealthy Roman elites could purchase slaves who "have no calves, or who are weasel-armed, or who have three eyes, or who are ostrich headed."[25] The imperial predilection for deformed individuals and slaves during the reigns of Claudius and Nero is confirmed by multiple sources, including Tacitus, Juvenal, and Suetonius. Tacitus writes that Claudius was intimate with Julius Paelignus, whom Tacitus describes as "despised alike for his stupid mind and contemptible body." Nero, we are told, filled his court with a number of "most dreadful monstrosities."[26] "Monster and emperors thus gravitated inevitably toward each other. Indeed, their exclusion from the world of the able-bodied made the deformed the ideal companions and confidants of emperors."[27]

Given that Paul may have been writing Philippians while imprisoned in the imperial household during the reign of either Claudius or Nero, it is certainly not beyond speculation that he was aware of the imperial household's predilection for deformed slaves. Could it be that his awareness of the abuse of such slaves provides a kind of metaphorical backdrop for his depiction of Christ taking on the form (μορφή) of a slave to then be exalted as *Kurios* (2:7)? Indeed, this lends another hue to theo-political readings in which the exaltation of Christ's name above all names (2:9) results in Christ receiving the title *kurios*, the Roman imperial title (2:11). If Christ's μορφή can be thought of in teratological terms, a

23. Garland, *Eye of the Beholder*, 46.
24. Garland, *Eye of the Beholder*, 47.
25. Garland, *Eye of the Beholder*, 47.
26. Garland, *Eye of the Beholder*, 48–49.
27. Garland, *Eye of the Beholder*, 49.

fascinating parallel can be found in Seneca's satirical *Apocolocyntosis*. In this work, when the emperor Claudius arrives at Mount Olympus for his apotheosis, his disfigurement shocks Hercules. Seneca writes that when Hercules saw:

> The monster's strange appearance and weird gait, and heard the hoarse and inarticulate voice of no earthly creature but such as might belong to a creature of the deep, he thought his thirteenth labour had come. On closer inspection, it turned out to be almost human (quasi homo). (5)[28]

The monstrous emperor, prior to his *apotheosis* is depicted as *quasi homo*. In contrast, Paul's apotheosis of Christ in the Christ hymn posits Christ not as *quasi homo*, but in *similitudenem hominum*. Of course, even calling the Christ hymn an apotheosis is not quite accurate because Paul begins by depicting Christ as being in the form of God (1:6) and then taking on the form of a slave. It is as slave that Christ is in the likeness (ἐν ὁμοιώματι; Phil 2:7) of a human being. For Paul, unlike for Aristotle—and apparently for Seneca as well—the human male form is *not* the standard of perfection, the standard of *kalokagathia*. In comparison to the form of God, for Paul the human form is equated with the form of the slave, the *kakos*, as it were. This is the key point for how one might read this text theologically from the perspective of disability studies. Paul's depiction of Christ in the Christ hymn does not prioritize a perfect human form. Paul's account not only does not accord with the widespread Greco-Roman physiognomic view of the perfect man, it undercuts the notion that less "well-formed" bodies are somehow deviant of some ideal *kalokagathia*. This would explain in part that, when given the choice to live in the flesh (ἐν σαρκί; Phil 1:22) and dying to be with Christ, Paul says that to be with Christ is far better (1:23). The human form itself implies brokenness.

This then is the theological key for understanding the language of friendship leading up to the Christ hymn. If being human

---

28. Following Garland, *Eye of the Beholder*, 51.

implies brokenness, if being human implies disability, having the same mind with Christ implies seeking not one's own advantage, but constantly finding ways to be a slave, and hence taking on the very form of disfigurement for others. At the conclusion of the Christ hymn Paul exhorts the Philippians to work out their own salvation in "fear and trembling" of a God who can enable (ὁ ἐνεργῶν; Phil 2:13) them both to will and be able to do (τὸ ἐνεργεῖν; Phil 2:13) the things that please God, just as, so to speak, God exalted and enabled the disabled Christ.

Friendship in Vanier

Vanier's notion of friendship and community are based in his moral philosophy. Vanier completed his doctoral dissertation in 1962 at the Catholic Institute of Paris on "Happiness as Principle and End of Aristotelian Ethics."[29] Following a close reading of Aristotle, Vanier posits the pursuit of happiness as the chief aim that all humans drive toward in their lives, indeed it is the keystone of human existence.[30] To become happy, to become deeply human, Vanier believes that Aristotle has laid out his ethics as a practical science that is based in human experience. As such, following Aristotle (see our discussion in chapter 1), friendship is the "pinnacle of life," the chief pursuit of the most highly fulfilled moral human being.[31] Friendship, however, is not pursued simply for the aim of pleasure or utility, things that benefit one's own self, but for the sake of the other. This other-centered friendship coalesces nicely with Paul's self-sacrificial theology of the cross in Phil 2. Vanier quotes Aristotle,

> It is true of the good man too that he does many acts for the sake of his friends and his country, and if necessary dies for them. . . . Rightly then is he thought to be good, since he chooses nobility before all else. But he may even give up actions to his friend; it may be nobler to become

29. Vanier, *Made for Happiness*, xii–xiii.
30. Vanier, *Made for Happiness*, 8.
31. Vanier, *Made for Happiness*, 69.

the cause of his friend's acting than to act himself. (*Nic. Eth.* 1169a17–34)[32]

One might best think of Vanier's L'Arche communities as workshops for practicing these kind of virtues. Living together, the disabled and the more abled members of the community practice the classical virtues as understood by Aristotle: courage and temperance, generosity and magnificence, good temper, amiability, veracity, sense of humor, magnanimity, and ultimately justice.[33] They also become places in which the virtue of friendship is learned and practiced, as members of the community learn to wonder together[34] through times of worship and contemplation, and of course grow both separately and together as practitioners of good in contemporary society. In a powerful way, Vanier's understanding of friendship and community is manifestly Aristotelian. His communities become workshops for applying Christian moral philosophy in deeply practical and constructive ways.

Vanier, however, does not simply blindly apply Aristotelian thought to the moral life of his communities. In his own appraisal of Aristotle, Vanier also dialectically engages with its pitfalls and blind spots. One of his chief critiques of Aristotle is the hierarchical nature of Aristotelian thought in relationship to friendship and the virtues. As we have noted numerous times already in this book, Aristotle thought that the virtues could only be fully perfected and achieved by privileged, high-status males. Perfect friendships, friendships that are practiced for the sake of friendship and are not based upon utility or pleasure, can only be shared between such equally high-status men. As Vanier notes, Aristotle does allow for women, slaves, and those of lesser status to practice virtue in their own limited ways. However, as a proponent for the disabled, Vanier finds it deeply problematic and shocking that Aristotle calls for "deformed" children to not be brought up by their parents, and calls for abortion of such embryos, if at all possible.[35]

32. Vanier, *Made for Happiness*, 159.

33. Vanier, *Made for Happiness*, 109–39.

34. Vanier, *Made for Happiness*, 77–108.

35. Vanier, *Made for Happiness*, 181.

This hierarchical ideal, as found in Aristotle, is deeply troubling for a man who has invested his life's work in the formation of communities in which the abled and disabled live together on more or less equal footing.

The problem, as Vanier sees it, is that Aristotle's fundamental definition of personhood is flawed. Vanier insists that "a person is defined not by his capacity to reason but by his capacity for relationship."[36] Here, Vanier's redefinition of personhood is deeply aligned with the Pauline understanding we laid out above. For Paul, the ideal human body is not the standard of perfection. Just as Paul rejects a kind of Greco-Roman *kalokagathia*, Vanier is rejecting Aristotelian notions of personhood that are based simply upon the capacity to reason. For both, it is the relational aspect—and the affective—that become the definition and standard for humanity. Instead, we express our true humanity—in Paul's language, we take on the form of the human being—in our capacity to relate to one another.

Conclusion

What does this mean for a reading of Paul, Vanier, and our understanding of friendship? Just as Christ's death, resurrection and exaltation are part of the universal metastory that Paul is telling in Phil 2:6–11, we can experience death, resurrection, and indeed exaltation as part of our common story too. I often tell my students that yes, I agree with Aristotle that human beings are political animals. However, human beings are also story-loving creatures. We dynamically experience a past, present, and imagined future, and we love to engage together with others in imaginative acts of what it means to be human. Similarly, Vanier rejects the static ideal of the Aristotelian universe, because for him, "by contrast the biblical vision is evolutionary. . . . People have a history. They walk beneath God's gaze and expect fulfillment of the promise He has made them. These people are focused on the future."[37] In our

36. Vanier, *Made for Happiness*, 181.
37. Vanier, *Made for Happiness*, 189.

storied reality, in a deep sense, all people have an opportunity to take on the form of Christ. All human experience is replete with the defective, broken, and vulnerable. Loneliness and separation are the baseline for human experience. Yet, according to Paul, because of what Christ did, we can live our lives with a storied promise. As we represent to one another Christ's broken bodies, holding through friendship the needs of the other above our own, we indeed begin to experience the wonder of the resurrected body in our communities.

This is precisely the dynamic that Vanier points to time and again as he shares in his writings experiences from his communities. This then is the Christian transformation of the Greco-Roman friendship ideal that we have seen expressed in various ways throughout the New Testament. Aristotle, according to Vanier, although holding up the significance of friendship, misses the mark by neglecting compassion.

> Through relationship with the poor or weak person or with the child, the heart, compassion, and goodness are awakened, and a new inner unity is established between body and soul. . . . Compassion engages the body and it is through the body that we draw nearer to others. We discover that the fragile person can help us undergo an inner transformation. We become more human, more welcoming, and more open to others.[38]

New Testament friendship and community are based in the recognition of our common human brokenness and vulnerability. The experience of such friendship and community enables humans to "make joy complete" (Phil 2:2) by living lives of meaning, purpose, and value.

---

38. Vanier, *Made for Happiness*, 188.

8

"Whoever Wishes to Be a Friend of the World . . ."

New Monasticism and an Interpretation of James's Friendship Ethos (Jas 4:4)

CHRISTIAN COMMUNITY SHOULD NOT be viewed as a simple panacea for the loneliness and isolation of contemporary life. The thesis of this book is that the New Testament writers adapted the language of Greco-Roman friendship to express the practices, ethos, and experience of their distinctive communities. These communities, however, were meant to stand in bold contrast to the world around them. James expresses it like this, "Friendship with the world is enmity with God" (4:4). Throughout the New Testament, and especially in James, Christian communities are called to question the injustice and call out the exploitation of the world, not provide a panacea to lonely and isolated rich people. Yet in a world of networked individualism, might a renewed understanding of friendship provide both community and a prophetic contrast to broken individuals who live in a world of greed and exploitation?

Isolation and the Search for Authentic Friendship in a World of Riches

Over the past couple of decades, the new monastic movement has attracted a fair share of young middle class white people who are searching for Christian community that is more authentic and challenging than the ones in which they grew up. Along with these kids, the communities of the new monastic movement comprise a cross-selection of folks from various races, classes, and social statuses. They also serve the underserved in the neighborhoods where they are formed, and offer prophetic challenges to church and world as a whole. In certain ways, new monastic communities live up to James's call to be distinctive, while challenging the brokenness and greed of the world. As a white male scholar and higher education professional, I possess considerable privilege, experienced in the comfort of worldly possessions. This comfort, at times, prevents me from experiencing authentic, rejuvenating Christian community. I too, like the young, white, middle class Christians who are seeking out the new monastic movement, yearn for authentic community. Before turning to a discussion of James and James's adaptation of the Greco-Roman friendship idiom, I would like to share some of my own story, particularly as it pertains to the quest for authentic community. I do so because some in my audience may too be familiar with the comfort and privilege of middle class America. They will also struggle with the cognitive and emotional dissonance that a life as rich Christians presents. While authentic Christian community is not meant as a panacea for the rich, could it provide an alternative vision of what it may mean to be Christian in a wealthy society? What follows is part of my quest for an answer to this question.

When I was a boy, growing up in the 1970s and '80s in Louisville, Kentucky, I remember my mother used to take me occasionally to congregational meetings of Brethren in Christ folks. They met regularly in one of the congregation member's homes. Very different from the large formal worship of the moderate Southern Baptist church in which we were members, I found the simple, quiet, spontaneous worship style of this little house church to be deeply soothing. Especially in my angst-ridden and questioning teen years, the occasional visits we made to this community refreshed my troubled soul. My mother, who grew up in Southeastern Pennsylvania, attended Brethren in Christ churches with her father, a man whose piety made a great impression upon me as a child. My grandfather, who had only the equivalent of a grammar school education, had much of the Bible memorized. Every other sentence from him was a Proverb or some other Bible verse. Working as a postman to send his children to college, he voraciously read not only the Bible, but from cover to cover each and every one of the textbooks that my mother and uncles and aunt brought home with them from college. His faith, though, was not only one of pious sentiment. My mother recalled how during the Depression there was often an extra plate at the evening dinner table for a stranger in need whom he had met in his work that day. Every Sunday he packed up his children and took them to the mission in downtown Philadelphia to hand out sandwiches and pour coffee for the homeless, more often than not bringing one or two of the men back with them to stay in the spare room they always had ready for unexpected guests at home. In these ways, I believe my grandfather modelled the kind of activist faith that, as we shall see, James was calling for.

After college in the late '80s and early '90s, I was struggling deeply. I knew I had a call to some kind of ministry. However, I struggled to square this call with what I had witnessed as ministry in the wealthy, suburban, moderate Baptist church I had grown up in. This was further complicated by discord and strife in the Southern Baptist Convention. Throughout the Southern Baptist Convention, fundamentalists and strict biblical literalists were taking over one seminary and missionary institution after another, firing or forcing out deeply faithful and committed professors, pastors, and missionaries, some of whom were personal friends of our family. I felt less and less comfortable in the denomination in which I had grown up. It was a lonely, alienating experience. I didn't have the language to express what I thought was wrong with the church. What's worse, I felt the alienation I was experiencing may somehow have been my fault. Perhaps in part it was. I sometimes struggle with holding my tongue when I see injustice, when I see social and (especially) ecclesial structures that are preventing folks from living into the fullness of life. Yes, my tongue sometimes gets me in trouble and isolates me from those whom I question. The prophetic life can sometimes be quite lonely. Perhaps it was ironic that I should find my call in the emptiness of that broken and alienated situation. Perhaps if I hadn't been in the desert, I wouldn't have heard the call at all.

The year after I graduated from college, I took on various odd jobs. I was especially drawn to service with those who were in some sense broken, marginalized, or ill. I worked as a house manager in a halfway house for people diagnosed with serious mental illness, and as a substitute teacher at the Kentucky School for the Blind. Working with visually and mentally impaired children during the day, and then going later in the afternoon to prepare dinner together with schizophrenics, to make sure chores were done, medicines were taken, and sleeping on a couch in the manager's office; all of this was deeply fulfilling for me. Somehow, during moments throughout the day, I sensed I was in contact with something that was at the same time both very vulnerable and deeply divine. It was around this time that a friend connected me with the Church of the Brethren, and their Brethren Volunteer Service. I was a volunteer for six months in a soup kitchen in Southeast Washington, DC. After that I served a tour of two years doing peace, justice, and reconciliation work in former East Berlin. These experiences provided me a renewed sense of church, as I experienced new friendships with homeless men and women in the belly of the beast of the US capitol, and reconciled with former cold war "enemies," some of whom had been leaders in the nonviolent candlelight campaign that originated in the ecumenical movement in East Germany and had spread into the protests that eventually broke open the Berlin Wall.[1] The church in socialism had combined with other move-

---

1. For a crisp introduction to the ecumenical movement that brought down the wall and a guidebook to community organizing and peacemaking,

ments in Poland, the Czech Republic, and in Hungary to unravel the iron curtain, and provide new freedoms to large populations throughout Eastern Europe. It was truly an inspiration for me to work with pastors who had participated in that movement. Moreover, I learned from them that they in turn had taken inspiration from a church movement spawned in a different era and different culture, the civil rights movement in the US South during the '60s, a movement about which I had learned almost nothing growing up in my wealthy, white, suburban Southern Baptist church.

After serving for two years in Berlin, I ended up staying another three, beginning my theological studies, continuing to work in churches and with disabled children. In addition, as I had time, I continued to be active in nonviolence, peace, and social justice movements. Now and again, especially in Germany, I visited, led workshops in, or had other kinds of contact with house churches in former East and West Germany. I have always admired the way that the house church movement meets members' needs for community, while providing space for spiritual growth, and engaging in social advocacy and relief for the poor and marginalized. In North America, new monasticism is a kind of house church movement in the contemporary church that beautifully captures the ethos of James's wisdom-infused friendship advice.

Wisdom, Authentic Activist Community, and Friendship in James

The letter of James is a prime example of a product of the early church in which the Greco-Roman friendship ethos is being explicitly turned on its head and applied to Christian community. Indeed, this is the only place in the New Testament where the Greek noun for friendship, ἡ φιλία, is being used (Jas 4:4). Johnson claims that in 2:23 and 4:4, James shows familiarity with the Greco-Roman *topos* on friendship.[2] While this may be the case,

---

see Stassen, *Just Peacemaking*.

2. Johnson, *Brother of Jesus*, 18.

there may be more evidence that James is using a wisdom literature *topos* on friendship that can be found in the Septuagint, especially in the Wisdom of Solomon and Ben Sirach.[3] The best place to look as a source for James's use of friendship might be in the friendship saying of Jesus that we discussed in chapter 2. The immediate context of Jas 4:1–10, in which the friendship saying occurs, is filled with allusions to Jesus sayings.[4] James 4:4, in which "friendship with the world" is contrasted with enmity with God, may be read as a recasting of Jesus' saying that the son of man is perceived as a "glutton and drunkard, and a friend of tax collectors and sinners" (Matt 11:19; Luke 7:34–35). Indeed, the sapiential themes in James provide a context for appropriately understanding what Jesus meant in the second part of his saying, that "wisdom is vindicated by her deeds."

The letter of James advocates for an activist faith that is grounded in divine wisdom. Its focus is social justice. These three themes, an activist faith, wisdom, and social justice are intertwined throughout the text, providing a solid context for the friendship sayings in 2:23 and 4:4. Wisdom, for James, resides on the divine end of a dialectic between worldly notions of status and success, and divine requirements of advocacy for the poor and oppressed. The poor and the oppressed, those marginalized by the practices of the wealthy and the elite, are the ones with whom one should be friends. Just as Jesus aligned with tax collectors and sinners, James is calling upon his community to align with the poor and dispossessed. For James, there is a clear dualism between the poor and

3. See especially Wis 7:14. See also Wis 8:18; Sir 6:17; 22:20; 25:1; 27:18. For an interesting example of a wisdom friendship *topos* that has similarities to the Greco-Roman *topos* on the importance of admonishment of friends, see Prov 25:10 LXX, which translates roughly in English, "Unless your friend reproaches you, your quarrelsomeness and enmity will not depart; but will be to you like death. Favor and friendship will free (you). Keep them for yourself so that you do not become despised, but guard your ways peaceably." For additional places where ἡ φιλία is used in LXX wisdom literature, see also Prov 10:12; 17:9; 19:7; 27:5.

4. For example Jas 4:2–3 may be referring to Matt 7:7 and Luke 11:9; Jas 4:9 to Matt 5:4 and Luke 6:21; while Jas 4:10 may be referring back to Matt 21:12 and Luke 14:11. See also Johnson, *Brother of Jesus*, 136–54.

rich, between the powerful and the marginalized, the elites and the disposables of society. An activist faith responds to this dualism by aligning, as a community, with the poor and marginalized. This then, for James, is the content of wisdom, because wisdom itself is associated with the divine, while rejecting the worldly and materialistic.

James's Notion of Proper Wisdom

The entire book of James reads more or less like a collection of wisdom sayings. It is difficult to discern any kind of sustained or structured argument for the work. The book's introduction underscores a pedagogical model, in which trials produce an endurance that leads toward perfection and maturity (1:2–3). The *telos* of that perfection is wisdom, σοφία, a quality that is given by God to those who ask for it in faith (1:5–6). The wisdom sayings in James, therefore, are targeted toward an audience that has experienced some trials, perhaps in the past; but his audience also appears to be patiently waiting for the coming of the Lord at a time of relative peace (5:7–12). It would not appear that the audience is under any kind of severe persecution. James recognizes that there is suffering, but also cheer (5:13) in his audience; illness, but also anointing (5:14); sin, but also those who are righteous (5:15–16). Such conditions, in which outside persecutions are minimal and there is relative stability within the community, are ideal for the development of a wisdom ethos. James's wisdom is the end goal of a distinctly Christian pedagogical practice. Such wisdom targets a congregation that is stable and maturing, has sufficient wealth, but also a fair number of members who are poor, and is relatively persecution free.

The Greek word for wisdom, σοφία, occurs four times in James. It occurs once in the introduction, as we have discussed, and three more times in 3:15–17; the adjective, σοφός, occurs once, only in 3:15. The words "wisdom" and "wise" come at the conclusion of a section in James about teaching and the mastery of the tongue. If teaching for James has a sapiential function in his community, he makes clear that only a few from the community should strive for this vocation (3:1). In the following verses, James launches into a discussion about how to control the tongue, the only one of its kind in the New Testament, but one which has extensive parallels in Greco-Roman moral thought and the LXX wisdom literature.[5] Expanding on the proverb in 1:26 that an unbridled tongue is deceptive and irreligious, James elevates control of the tongue as a practice that is perfected by the moral teacher, indeed making him a perfect man (τέλειος ἀνὴρ; 3:2), someone who is able to hold in check the whole body. After a section highlighting the possibility of doing great damage with the tongue (3:5–7), James comes back to the character trait associated with the proper use of the tongue: a gentleness that is born of wisdom.

James contrasts the prized gentleness born of wisdom with bitter envy and selfish ambition (3:14). Indeed, the dualism set forth in these verses continues at least until 4:10. The words envy, ζῆλος, and selfish ambition, ἐριθεία, occur as a pair in this section twice, once in 3:14 and again in 3:16. They are associated with other "earthly, unspiritual," and even "devilish" (3:15) character traits including boastfulness, mendacity, indeed disorder and wickedness of every kind (3:16). Such character traits are the source for conflicts and disputes in James's community (4:1–2). Mirroring 3:15–16, James pairs the noun πόλεμος, conflict, with μάχη, quarrel, in 4:1, and repeats their verb cognates in 4:2. Similarly, this allows him to fill a word field with related character traits, including craving (4:1), covetousness, and indeed murder (4:2). Johnson, therefore, I think is correct in seeing 3:13—4:10 as a single exegetical unit perhaps related to a Greco-Roman *topos* on envy.[6]

---

5. For a discussion of the Greco-Roman parallels, see Johnson, *Brother of Jesus*, 155–67. See also the connection between education, wisdom, and the tongue in Sir 4:24; the connection between appropriate control of the tongue and friendship in 6:5; the power of the tongue to do damage in Sir 5:13, 14; 19:16; 20:18; 22:27; 25:8; 28:17, 18, 26; 51:2, 5, 6; as well as the power to control and manage the tongue in Sir 32:8; 37:18; 51:22.

6. Johnson, *Brother of Jesus*, 182–201. Johnson's proposal certainly merits serious consideration. I would argue that it may be a bit of a stretch to see this connected to a *topos* περὶ φθόνος, if the linchpin of the argument relies too

In this passage, earthly envy is contrasted with "wisdom that is from above" (3:17) and gentleness (3:13). Here James has chiastically arranged negative "earthly" character traits associated with conflict in 3:15–16 and 4:1–2 around positive character traits that come "from above" and are associated with peace in 3:17–18. Indeed, the word or cognate for peace, εἰρήνη, occurs three times in 3:17–18. So being peaceable, sewing peace, and making peace are associated with character traits such as being holy, gently compliant, full of mercy and good fruits, unwavering, and genuine (3:17).

By contrasting these positive and negative character traits, James is setting forth his definition of friendship. The dialectic between worldly and divine provides the context for James's statement about friendship in chapter 4: "Adulterers, Do you not know that worldly friendship is divine enmity? The one who wishes to be a friend of the world, sets himself up as an enemy of God" (4:4). For James, being a friend of God is the pinnacle of being righteous and faithful. Hence in 2:23, Abraham is characterized as a friend of God. Here, James seems to be referring to a later tradition in which Abraham comes to be viewed as a friend of God (Isa 41:8; 2 Chr 20:7). This later tradition may reflect the notion that wisdom makes one a friend of God. This is explicit in the beautiful encomium to wisdom in Wis 7:24–27:

> For wisdom is more mobile than any motion; because of her pureness she pervades and penetrates all things. For she is a breath of the power of God, and a pure emanation of the glory of the Almighty; therefore nothing defiled gains entrance into her. For she is a reflection of eternal light, a spotless mirror of the working of God, and an image of his goodness. Although she is but one, she can do all things, and while remaining in herself, she renews all things; *in every generation she passes into holy souls and makes them friends of God*, and prophets; for God loves nothing so much as the person who lives

heavily upon reading the word φονεύετε (4:2), you murder, as φθονεῖτε, you are envious. While φθονεῖτε makes better sense in the context of the sentence, there is no manuscript evidence for such an emendation, even if Erasmus suggested it.

with wisdom. She is more beautiful than the sun, and
excels every constellation of the stars. Compared with
the light she is found to be superior, for it is succeeded
by the night, but against wisdom evil does not prevail.
(Wis 7:24–30)

In this tradition, wisdom is viewed as both the power and
breath of God (7:24), reflecting the image of divine goodness
(7:25). Like Jas 3:13—4:10, wisdom here functions on one end of a
dialectic, aligned with God, light, and goodness, but against darkness and evil (7:29–30). As such, she will move into (μεταβαίνω)
holy souls (ψυχὰς ὁσίας; 7:27), in each generation. The same concept, that the Spirit comes to dwell in humans, is reflected in Jas
4:5. In James we also see a similar dialectic, in that resisting the
devil (4:7) is equated to submission to God. Drawing near to God,
cleansing hands and purifying hearts, allows God to draw near to
us. Just as James is admonishing his community to be peaceable
and gentle in 3:17–18, in 4:7–10, he enjoins them to submit with
purity, brokenness, and humility to God's presence. This makes
them into friends of God.

In other respects, the LXX wisdom tradition resembles standard Greco-Roman tropes that could be found in, for example,
Cicero or Plutarch.[7] Sirach 6:16 concludes a brief section on advice
related to friendship with the claim that those who fear the Lord
will know how to properly direct their friendship. James provides
no instructions for how one might properly pursue human friendship. Unlike Sir 6:5–13 (and Plutarch, *Amic. Mult.* 2.1), there is no
advice to have only a few friends who have been thoroughly tested.
Missing is any discussion of faithless or fickle friends, flatterers, or
those who cannot be trusted (6:8–13). Nor is there the view that
faithful friends can provide a life-saving medicine (6:16), or that
friends can be a shelter (6:14) or priceless treasure (6:14–15). The
humble, peaceable, unwaveringly devout, holy and gentle person
who is considered to be a friend of God in James operates in a
context that is completely different from that of the person who

---

7. *Amic; Amic. mult.* See discussion of Plutarch and Cicero in chapter 2
above.

hopes to advance in the court school in Sirach or Proverbs, or who is a wealthy and powerful ruler who must discriminate among counselors in Plutarch's discussion on flattery and friendship. As we shall see in the following sections, James's congregational context determines the contours and meaning of Christian friendship. In James, friendship entails faithful activism for the poor and the marginalized.

The Rich and Poor in James

For many rich believers in the North American or Western European twenty-first century context, James is not merely a challenge, it is a condemnation. James's prophetic-like critique of the rich forms an *inclusio* for the book as a whole. It begins with a prophecy in 1:10–11 that the rich, in their busy lives, will be "brought low," will wither and disappear like flowers under scorching heat. The book concludes with a condemnation of the rich in 5:1–5. They are enjoined to "weep and wail" for the miseries that await them (5:1). Their possessions, clothes, silver, and gold will be destroyed (5:1–2), used as rusting evidence against them (5:3). Making a wonderful play on imagery associated with eating, James claims that the rich who luxuriously feasted so much as to fatten their hearts on a day of slaughter (5:5) will now see their rusted gold and silver eat their own flesh like fire (5:3). Indeed, the rich are blamed for the condemnation and murder of the "righteous one," who has not resisted them. While he does not use this language, the implication for James is that the rich are indeed antichrists, who are awaiting destruction in the end of times.

Along with this condemnation of the rich, we also see a reversal in this *inclusio* of categories between rich and poor. The poor who have labored in the fields of the rich, whose wages have been garnered, are the ones whom the Lord of hosts hears (5:4). Indeed, echoing the reversal in Jesus' Sermon on the Mount, the lowly will be raised up, while the rich will be brought low (5:5). The second person admonition in 5:1, "Come on, rich folk (οἱ πλούσιοι), cry," confirms that at least a portion of James's audience consisted of wealthy individuals. Other parts of James's audience are cautioned against currying favor with the rich. James describes a situation in which a beautifully dressed rich person is offered the best seats in church, while the poor and shabbily dressed are relegated to where there is standing room only, or to sit on the floor. Here again James invokes a clear reversal: "Listen, beloved brothers, did not God choose the poor in the world as rich in faith, and heirs of the kingdom which he promised to those who love him" (2:5)? The poor, then, represent those in his audience whom James considers to be "rich in faith" and "heirs of the kingdom." This reversal between rich and poor therefore resembles James's dialectic between the friends of God—those who are humble, peaceable, and devout—and their opposite, the friends of the world—those who are self-serving, boastful, mendacious, wicked, and conflict-aroused. For James, then, friendship with God is not achieved simply through embracing the poor. Practicing proper friendship in James's community requires an all-encompassing embrace of poverty and a rejection of the rich and powerful.

James's warnings to the rich and moderately well-off in his audience reflect not just his concerns about social and material injustice. For James, neglect of the poor by the Christian community reveals a deep flaw in the experience and practice of faith. James offers the example of a believer (brother or sister; ἀδελφὸς ἢ ἀδελφὴ) in the community who is living naked and lacks adequate daily nourishment (2:15). James criticizes the actions of wealthier members in his community (someone from among you; τις ἐξ ὑμῶν) as worthless, when they do no more than simply utter warm platitudes instead of supplying the poor person's bodily needs (τὰ ἐπιτήδεια τοῦ σώματος; 2:16). For James, such empty encouragement neither serves Christian community, nor is representative of a healthy and active faith. A healthy faith is expressed by building authentic community that challenges injustice. Interpreting 2:16 through Luther's hermeneutical lens of "works righteousness" has proven deeply corrosive for much of the Protestant faith. James is not so much advocating works righteousness here, as he is criticizing an unaccountable (2:10), even dead (2:17), faith, a faith that is skewed toward apathy, platitudes, and indeed, transgression of the love command that should condition all Christian faith (2:8). James's key insight is that truly loving one's neighbor as oneself requires an activist faith.

Activism as a Sign of Faith

Peppered throughout James are exhortations to an activist faith. In 1:22, James famously calls upon his audience to "be doers of the word, and not only hearers who are deceiving themselves." But what does James mean by "word" (λόγος) here? Although it is not developed in a full philosophical sense, James's understanding of λόγος somewhat resembles Stoic ideas of a divine will that orders the universe. In 1:18, James contends that, acting "according to his plan" (βουληθεὶς), God "gave birth to us through the word of truth (λόγῳ ἀληθείας), so that we might become, in some kind, the first fruits of his creatures."

This verse explicates two key concepts associated with James's understanding of λόγος. First, λόγος is an expression of God's will. This is important for understanding James's use of the wisdom tradition. If the divine will, the divine plan, is part of the cosmic order, wisdom ideas, such as those found in James, may flourish. Wisdom, at least the kind of wisdom that can be found in James, Proverbs, as well as Wisdom and Sirach, depends on a conception of the cosmos that is stable, ordered, and aligned with God's will. Secondly, the λόγος is innate in human beings. Unlike in the Johannine writings, we can find no evidence that James is operating with a christological understanding of the λόγος. The λόγος, rather, is that principle through which God's will becomes manifest through our living, as we represent the "first fruits," ἀπαρχή, of the new eschatological order (1:18). Secondly, the λόγος, for James is implanted, ἔμφυτος, within human souls, and can either be received or rejected by humans (1:21). However, believers can only receive the λόγος through their own humility. When they do so, it has the power to save their souls (1:21). For James, therefore, becoming doers of the λόγος means to express the same kind of humility associated with friendship with God, in alignment with the will and plan of God.

Friendship as Community Activism

For James, activist faith is directly tied to deeds of social holiness. "Pure and undefiled religion before God the father is this: to visit the orphans and the widows when they are suffering, and to keep oneself unstained by the world" (1:27). James expands upon this in 2:14–17. The well-known maxim in Jas 2:17 that faith without works is dead is contextualized by the believer's engagement of the poor (2:14–16). As discussed above, seeing a fellow believer naked or hungry and not doing anything constructive to address those needs indicates for James a serious flaw in faith. James's turn to the Abraham and Rahab stories to justify his demand for an activist faith cannot be separated from his concern for the poor in his community. With a straight face, one could almost claim that James is the first to embrace a liberationist hermeneutic. For James, God indeed listens to the cries of the poor and those dispossessed through unjust economic systems (5:4). God's preferential option for the poor is expressed through the believer's activist faith that is undertaking action to concretely meet the needs of the widows, orphans, naked, and hungry.

Friendship, Community Activism, and the New Monastic Movement

In today's world, where might one find the kind of authentic community that is actively advocating for justice and practicing lived solidarity with the poor? What would that look like for those of us, like myself, who are coming from a context of privilege and soul-sucking comfort? One of the key insights that Jonathan Wilson-Hartgrove offers, as he discusses the necessity for the new monastic movement, is that it is hard to be a faithful Christian in the North American context today.[8] He relates the story how he, as a young

8. Wilson-Hartgrove, *New Monasticism*, 11.

congressional staffer living and working in Washington, DC, went to lunch one day and almost tripped over a homeless man begging in Union Station. Feeling guilty for ignoring this man's needs, he ran back to his apartment, picked up an evangelistic Gospel tract, wrapped a twenty dollar bill around it and returned to give it to the man. People like me, who grew up with a comfortable suburban Christianity but want to take seriously James's advice not to ignore the poor among them, are struggling to find truth and authenticity in American Christianity. Young Christians, whether they are participating in Hartgrove's "School for Conversion," Shane Claiborne's "Simple Way," or Elaine Heath's "Missional Wisdom" movement, are finding friendships in intentional communities in which a sense of authentic Christianity is possible.[9] Whether they are there just to spend a gap year, or are committing to longer term stays, the houses founded by these movements offer communities in which folks can share not only common possessions, but a commitment to the poor around them. As James cautions the rich Christians of his day, the members participating in new monasticism are making commitments not to ignore the poor among them.

New Monasticism in North America

New monasticism is a North American movement that is expressed in a rich variety of local forms, depending on the mission and location of the community, the ethnic and denominational makeup of its participants, and in part the vision and direction of its leadership. Some, like the Simple Way in Philadelphia, are embedded in what many would consider blighted (or formerly

9. Reflecting on his upbringing in the church in East Tennessee, Shane Claiborne summarizes the predicament the church faces with regard to youth eloquently: "I remain convinced to this day that if we continue to lose young people in the church, it won't be because we made the gospel too hard but because we made it too easy. We will lose them not because the foosball table was broken or we didn't have the latest Xbox game in the youth room but because we didn't dare them to take Jesus seriously and connect the gospel to the world we live in." Claiborne, *Irresistible Revolution*, 41.

blighted) urban neighborhoods. In fact, the story of the Simple Way is inspiring. An eclectic group of idealistic college students got together with their homeless neighbors to squat in an abandoned church, and eventually purchase an abandoned building for their mother-house.[10] Since their founding in 1998, the Simple Way has expanded to include about a dozen properties, including a community garden, green space, housing, educational space, and even retail. The Simple Way has a permanent community of about a dozen members, as well as dozens of others who have come to the community from outside, or returned to the community for shorter transitional periods.

Another organization, the Missional Wisdom Foundation,[11] has in the past years experimented by founding a dozen networked communities in the Dallas Fort Worth area. The Epworth Project, borrowing its name from the birthplace of John and Charles Wesley and the church where their father, Samuel Wesley, was rector, includes small communities of undergraduate and graduate students, adults, and other residents who live intentionally according to a community rule for a transitional period of between two to four years. The Epworth Project includes a variety of different living spaces: purchased homes, rented apartments, and renovated parsonages. Communities in the Epworth Project each have an overseer, follow a regular and orderly daily devotional life, and are bound to a rule of life that "is based on the United Methodist baptismal covenant, which calls for commitments around prayers, presence, gifts, service, and witness." Each house sets its mission based upon its local context, whether that is to homeless, elderly, lonely, differently abled, or other local people in need.[12]

Neither the Simple Way nor the Missional Wisdom Foundation seek to supplant or displace the local church. Heath and Duggins, two of the principle leaders in the Missional Wisdom

10. http://www.thesimpleway.org.

11. https://www.missionalwisdom.com.

12. https://static1.squarespace.com/static/58dd921e5016e1eaf6880878/t/ 59663982725e25d0a6862a09/1499871618219/600+words+on+the+MWF+E pworth+Project+PDF.pdf

Foundation, have authored a guidebook of sorts to individuals and congregations in the United Methodist denomination who might wish to start a community of their own.[13] Although these communities incorporate regular devotions and worship as a part of their rule of life, they are encouraged to connect with and even in some cases be sponsored by local congregations. The idea is that they will spur and inspire local congregations to missional service in their context, while local congregations will bind these communities to ecclesial structures and denominational oversight. Indeed, for Duggins, "building new types of Christian community does not require the destruction of the old. It may be necessary to reallocate resources and update priorities, but that can be done within a framework of healthy respect for tradition."[14]

One such example is the Haw Creek Community, which the Missional Wisdom Foundation is building around a historic church, Bethesda United Methodist Church, in a suburb of Asheville. When I visited the church with Larry Duggins in 2015, I found that it had a worshipping community of less than a dozen people, and a sanctuary and Sunday school wing that was built or last renovated sometime during the church's heyday decades past. There was a quilting room, a dark fellowship hall with linoleum tile floor and metal folding chairs, Sunday school rooms that had not been updated in years, older bathrooms, carpet throughout; just what one might expect to find in a decaying and dying church. When I came, I parked in the lot that was facing the cemetery and beyond that the neighborhood elementary school. I was careful not to park near the sign that made it explicitly clear that parents were not to use the parking lot to pick up their children from the school, for fear that my car might be towed. When Larry walked me through the space, he shared his vision with me of creating a co-working space, remodeling the sanctuary and the Sunday school wing, and creating lots of ways for the neighborhood to come together as a community.[15] I thought he was crazy.

13. Heath and Duggins, *Missional, Monastic, Mainline.*

14. Duggins, *Together,* 35.

15. For a brief discussion of his plans, see Duggins, *Together,* vii–viii.

As I visited the church three years later, I was deeply impressed by how the vision of the Missional Wisdom Foundation (MWF) was able to shape both the church and its surrounding community. Part of the success lies in honoring the tradition. Before any renovations took place, the MWF took care to create a room in the church where archival materials, keepsakes, and other artifacts from the church's history and tradition could be accessed. This enabled the congregation members to see that MWF valued their history and identity as a church. Assured that their community was not going to be lost or forgotten, they were better able to see the vision of the MWF as continuing the centuries of service to the community. The efforts of the MWF would align with the tradition of the church as a space for community in the Haw Creek area.

In shaping the vision for Haw Creek, Duggins is operating from the understanding that people form community around four different areas: workplace, food and table, children's school, and affinity groups.[16] The renovations at Haw Creek fall along those lines.

First, MWF renovated the Bethesda's fellowship hall into a light-filled, beautifully open co-working space. Here, people who work from home or who are entrepreneurs can come and experience community while they work at the same place together. Upstairs, Sunday school rooms were renovated into smaller breakout rooms for appointments or teleconferencing.

Secondly, MWF put in an industrial kitchen that can be rented by start-ups, caterers, and other cooks who need a licensed space out of which to operate one or two days per week, but cannot afford a kitchen of their own. This emphasis on food naturally builds community. In MWF's co-working space in Dallas, it is not uncommon for the cooks renting the kitchen to share samples with those in the co-working space, building community and creating more business, and even sometimes paving the way for near collaborative ventures. In addition, MWF put in a large community garden in front of the parsonage, making fresh food available to

16. Duggins, *Together*, 35–37.

the neighborhood, and providing a work space for groups visiting the parsonage for spiritual formation retreats. Aligned with this vision is also the large free range chicken coop and well-tended beehives in the back.

In addition, the sign prohibiting parents from picking up their children from school has been replaced with a sign inviting parents to do so. A playground, nature path to the school, and other attractions (chicken coop, etc.) have been added so that the parents and their children can get a small walk in nature before and after school. Ideally, the parents will be able to drop in on the co-working space for a cup of coffee and some breathing room, after dropping off the kids.

Finally, the activities of the MWF have spawned a variety of affinity groups. The church's quilting group now has its own room in the community parsonage, and a neighborhood group has formed around the beehives, with an expanded focus on ensuring the well-being of all types of pollinators in the area. The MWF is finding other ways to reach affinity groups by offering Taize, yoga, and other opportunities. Meanwhile, although meeting in the parsonage while renovations to the sanctuary took place, the congregation and its weekly average worship attendance has quintupled in size.

The work of the MWF at places like Haw Creek does not simply provide a panacea for lonely, rich, and isolated suburban Americans. It also may not address issues of race or social injustice directly. However, it may provide a place of deep local connection for those of us so whose lives and experiences have been uprooted by the experience of networked individualism. Those of us who experience networked individualism as an acute loss of social capital may find, in such localized expressions of community, the kinds of healthy friendships and communities that have long been lost in the isolating suburbs of wealthy upper-middle-class America. In some ways, new monasticism may point the way toward a life that can be far richer, even in its simplicity.

The Marks of New Monasticism

While the forms of individual communities may vary, some members of the new monastic movement have acknowledged an ethos that is shared among them. In 2004, a group of folks associated with new monasticism throughout North America came together to outline the shape and common features of their movement, regardless of the diversity of its individual forms. What they came up with were "12 Marks of a New Monasticism." They are:

1. Relocation to the abandoned places of Empire.

2. Sharing economic resources with fellow community members and the needy among us.

3. Hospitality to the stranger.

4. Lament for racial divisions within the church and our communities, combined with the active pursuit of a just reconciliation.

5. Humble submission to Christ's body, the church.

6. Intentional formation in the way of Christ and the rule of the community along the lines of the old novitiate.

7. Nurturing common life among members of the intentional community.

8. Support for celibate singles alongside monogamous married couples and their children.

9. Geographical proximity to community members who share a common rule of life.

10. Care for the plot of God's earth given to us along with support of our local communities.

11. Peacemaking in the midst of violence and conflict resolution within communities along the lines of Matt 18.

12. Commitment to a disciplined contemplative life.

What is remarkable about these markers is how much they share with the vision and ethos of James. In their entirety, they reflect the activist expression of faith that is central to James's wisdom teaching. As a whole, they describe for a contemporary community what it means to "be doers of the word and not merely hearers" (1:22) and that "faith without works is dead" (2:27). Furthermore, with their commitment to not only seeing the plight of, but also serving the needs of neighbors in their local communities (marks 1, 2, 3, 4, 9, 10, and 11), they are clearly committed to correcting the flaw pointed out by James of rich Christians ignoring the poor (2:15–16). These marks, especially those concerned with racial reconciliation (4), peacemaking (11), and the environment (10) are indications of a deep commitment to an active engagement with the kind of social justice that is at the heart of James's wisdom teaching.

One of the other marks of new monasticism is the nurturing of common life in an intentional community (7), especially one that cultivates disciplined spirituality (12). In many respects, the new monastic movement of the twenty-first century not only catches but enhances James's rhyme and rhythm with respect to friendship. Individual members of new monastic communities may indeed experience a depth of deeply fulfilling personal relationships and renewed sense of friendship. One should not look to these communities, however, as fulfilling the sole purpose of providing solace and companionship for lost and lonely souls. Indeed, given the often complex and difficult dynamics inherent to living together intentionally, emotionally needy and personally broken individuals may be least suitable for the challenges and struggles of everyday life in such communities.

As I have stated throughout this chapter, new monastic communities should not be viewed as idyllic spiritual panaceas for lonely and rich American Christians. As we have discussed above, James redefines friendship as expressing faithful activism for the poor and the marginalized. Only those who engage in an activist faith that is committed to social justice can become, for James, friends of God. Furthermore, James contrasts the virtues of the friends of God with whatever worldly markers of success, power, or wealth that might be associated with our imagination of success. Nurturing spirituality and a common life is not the sole aim of new monasticism. These communities express a revitalized notion of friendship. This friendship is grounded in common life. It shares causes with the poor and broken. It seeks out locations in the neglected backwaters of a wasteful society, one that has been ravaged by the excesses of twenty-first century hyper-capitalism. The friendship practices of new monasticism take seriously a form of wisdom that embraces Jesus' love and preferential option for the poor, the broken, and the marginalized in society. This friendship submits to purity, brokenness, and humility in God's presence. These friends see themselves and greet others as children of God, human beings who are implanted with the Word of God. Most importantly, members of new monastic communities express acts of friendship daily through a combination of kindness, sharing possessions, providing hospitality, and engaging in radical social action for the poor.

9

A Biblical Theology of Friendship

FRIENDSHIP IS UNIVERSAL. ALL humans, regardless of where or when they live, have a need to experience and express friendship. When Aristotle recognizes that human beings are political animals, he in part is recognizing that we are made for friendship. The expression, purpose, and experience of friendship, therefore, are topics that hold profound significance for all humans everywhere. I embarked on the study of friendship many years ago while working on my doctoral dissertation at Princeton Theological Seminary. PhD programs can be notoriously socially isolating. Studying Luke's use of Greco-Roman friendship language in Acts provided deep meaning for me, not necessarily because I was socially isolated, but because I came to recognize just how flawed and deeply in need of authentic friendships human beings can be. Studying the narrative summaries of Acts 2:41–47 and 4:32–35 helped me to see how Luke recognized the importance of friendship for individuals in his own society. Luke offers a narrative portrayal of friendship in these passages. By placing God in the center of Christian community and depicting experiences of deep joy, gladness, and fellowship to those who participate in it, I theorized that Luke was responding to a narrative deficit of imagination regarding friendship among his late-first century audience. I also recognized that his portrayals can stimulate our imaginations. Luke's story about the early Christian community, in this sense, was a theological response to a deeply felt and widely experienced human need. I consider myself privileged to have had the opportunity to explore how Luke told this story, while considering the implications for reading Luke's narrative theologically and ethically for today.

Basic Presuppositions for New Testament Theology

In this concluding chapter, I invite you to join me to think a little more about how the different conceptions of friendship offered by New Testament writers might fit together as parts of a cohesive and coherent biblical theology. As I do so, I would also like to reflect how twenty-first century interpreters might engage in the practice and discipline of biblical theology. So by way of conclusion, as I pull it all together, I intend to offer a few brief reflections, proposals, and limitations for the practice of biblical theology.

Limitations of Biblical Theology

In this book, I have not undertaken anything nearly so grand as to attempt a comprehensive biblical theology. My interest, instead, has been focused almost solely on the language of friendship, and how it was articulated and adapted separately in a group of passages selected from various books of the New Testament. In part, my procedure was purposeful. I am skeptical that a coherent, cohesive, and expansive biblical theology of the New Testament can be undertaken that does not either ignore or forcefully harmonize the distinctive and diverse voices of the New Testament. What we have in the New Testament is neither one voice, nor one theology, but multiple genres in which various authors engage different communities and their concerns with a rich variety of theological expressions of Jesus Christ and his significance for humanity. If one were to undertake a biblical theology of the New Testament, one would need to give voice to this diversity.

The hermeneutical difficulties that weigh against the task of writing a New Testament theology make its possibility even harder to conceive. First, an interpreter seeking to write a biblical theology that is sensitive to the diverse historical contexts out of which the individual writings of the New Testament emerged would have to fully understand and grasp those historical contexts in the first place. This is not only a herculean task, it is also, to a degree, one that relies upon circular reasoning. Much of the historical and cultural background for the individual New Testament writings can only be gleaned from a reconstruction of that history provided by a close reading of the documents themselves. Biblical scholars are often not clear that the premises they bring to the internal clues provided by the New Testament documents may skew the conclusions they draw from them. We simply do not understand enough about ancient Greco-Roman and Mediterranean culture to know with much certainty whether the conclusions we are drawing provide us an accurate picture of the communities out of which the New Testament documents emerged. Building a theology based upon such premises is a risky business, and as Schweitzer cautioned, it can be a complete "disaster." Biblical scholars pursuing such a course are likely to find their own thoughts and imagination in the history they reconstruct.[1]

Even if a biblical theologian could draw conclusions about a New Testament theology, the difficulty arises that such a theology may not relate to the needs, perceptions, or problems of more than one reading community. While we are beginning to hear fresh voices, biblical scholarship continues to largely reflect Eurocentric, mostly male, and economically privileged viewpoints. Such a reading community no doubt exists. Nevertheless, I think it is incumbent upon contemporary interpreters to realize that engaging

---

1. "We have made Jesus speak another language to our time than that which he really used. In the process we ourselves have been enfeebled, and have robbed our own thoughts of their vigour in order to project them back into history and make them speak to us out of the past. It is nothing less than a disaster for modern theology that it mixes history with everything and ends by being proud of the skill with which it finds its own thoughts again in the past." Schweitzer, *Quest*, 480.

the Word of God theologically is taking place in a richly diverse world with any number of often contrasting perceptions, norms, and indeed, notions of reality. I remain skeptical that a given interpreter can fully or authentically give voice to the perceptions and preconceptions of interpreters from other cultural backgrounds. Nevertheless, I do believe that it is possible for me to make room in my interpretation for the imagination of other interpreters to fill my theology with their own impressions, creativity, and assumptions that may be derived from their own or others' cultural perspectives.

Thematically Oriented

The prolegomena I have briefly laid out in these few paragraphs shape my view of biblical theology. They also provide both an explanation and rationale for this current project. In this book, I have attempted to do biblical theology from a thematic perspective. As I contend above, friendship, as a theme, is a universal concern for all humans, regardless of their culture, time, or place. At the same time, various cultures, times, and places have given rise to a rich diversity of understandings of friendship. If one is going to write a book of biblical theology, I would advise selecting one theme, such as friendship, that has both universal application as well as a rich diversity of cultural expressions. One can imagine how a biblical theology of the New Testament might undertake such themes as human loss, reconciliation, birth/rebirth, hope, sin, forgiveness, conversion, and the like.

Culturally Embedded

In addition to being thematically oriented, this book has engaged in a narrative ethical reading of different biblical passages, relating them to the needs, peculiar perspectives, and concerns of a contemporary community, group, or issue. I briefly laid out in my introduction how narrative ethics proceeds by examining the biblical passage itself, and ethical concern that is embedded in the historical context in and for which the text was originally written, as well as engaging hermeneutically a contemporary community. Narrative ethics does not necessarily provide solutions to contemporary ethical dilemmas. Nor does it even overcome the historiographic problem of reconstructing ancient ethical concerns and assumptions. Instead, it captures the ways a given text might enliven and enrich the ethical imaginations of contemporary communities, inspiring them to seek out ways of relating that are life-giving and true to the biblical faith. Engaging each of the passages in this way reflects the fundamental idea that biblical theology must start in the realm of the practical. Biblical theology must in its inception be correlational. It must start from the ethical needs and experience of the communities that might read or engage the biblical text. Too often the guild of theological scholarship has begun with the abstract, started with the realm of theological ideas, propositionally formed through engagement with the biblical text, and then moved to description of ethical ideas. The method and proposal of this book is that biblical theology must start by engaging the Bible directly with the ethical experience of distinct communities and their needs. Its approach, informed by critical biblical readings of the text, is necessarily correlational.

Each of the chapters in this book, therefore, has staked out a reading perspective from a distinctive space, experience, or community: social media and online friendships, racial reconciliation in Mississippi and the US South, youth in the contemporary North American context, US veterans struggling with PTSD, communities of disability, and the movement of new monasticism. In each case I have taken a passage or passages from the Synoptic Gospels, Luke, Acts, John, Philippians, and James and sought to exploit those places where contemporary experience echoes the tone, rhythm, and melody of the friendship theology in each of these works. As such, I hope that the little biblical theology of friendship I have offered here sounds more like a jazz improvisation, staying true to the melody where I can find it, following the chord changes as they go alone, and incorporating the voices and intonations of fellow musicians, with the hopes that my voice might stimulate imaginative responses. What follows here is a brief summary of what such an improvisational biblical theology might intone.

Jesus, Friendship, and a Starting Point for New Testament Theology

Rudolf Bultmann is famous for making the claim that Jesus' message was the mere presupposition for New Testament theology, rather than a part of it.[2] On the face of it, his claim makes sense. Getting behind the Gospels' theological portrayals of Jesus' own thought and life requires significant critical discernment. Shaping a picture of Jesus' own theology can also generate considerable speculation. My theological work in this book, however, operates on two essential premises. First, while I agree about the dangers of speculation in reconstructing a thorough account of the historical Jesus' theology, I do believe that his individual sayings and the record of his actions can be placed in the historical context of first century Palestine and the wider Greco-Roman world to yield at least some thematic aspects of his theology. In this book, I have identified Jesus' saying on friendship and placed it within the context of his ministry in Palestine, as well as among the thinkers of the Greco-Roman world. Thus, while one may not be able to distill and reconstruct a full theological understanding of the historical Jesus, I do believe we can make some assumptions thematically about how Jesus thought about specific issues, in this case friendship.

Jesus' ministry to outcasts and undesirables in his community also verifies his claims regarding the potential of boundary breaking behavior in the kingdom of God. Jesus's theology seems to have guided him to engage in friendships with sinners, tax collectors, those on the margins of society, persons who were broken by disease, ritual contamination, and demon possession. They were in many ways isolated from their family, friends, and

2. Bultmann, *Theology of New Testament*, 1:1.

neighbors. In Jesus' theology, God has a preferential option for the broken, the misfits, and the outsiders, those who have nothing to offer in return. In Jesus' Kingdom of God, those who least expect or deserve it can become friends of God. In comparison, Greco-Roman thinkers excluded the possibility of authentic friendships between high and low status individuals, and between humans and gods; such friendships would have been strictly excluded. Jesus, on the other hand, makes the expression of such friendship the centerpiece of his kingdom building activity. In Jesus' kingdom, God actively desires friendship with the broken, the outcast, and the ignored.

There is also considerable continuity between Jesus' own boundary breaking friendship activities, and the theology of friendship that we see developed in the Gospels, Acts, Paul, and James. The authors of the New Testament received the tradition of Jesus' boundary breaking friendship behavior and developed it further as a way of expressing both their Christology and ecclesiology. John's focus on the idea that Jesus would lay down his life for his friends indicates just how important friendship theology was for understanding the implications of Jesus' death and resurrection. Jesus died willingly in order to create a community of friends, a group that is radically separate from the surrounding world. Because of their shared experience, possibly the shared trauma of persecution, this group of "insiders" has deep and essential bonds that outsiders cannot entirely comprehend. Paul's theology, on the other hand, views the cruciform participation in community as a form of friendship, a friendship that exposes one's own weakness and vulnerabilities in order to experience God at work, bolstering and building up others in the process. Similarly, in the Synoptic Gospels, understanding Jesus' identity and kingdom teaching leads one to recognize that reconciliation with one's enemies is possible as an expression of the radical experience of Jesus' friendship ethos of reaching out to the other. However, key to one's own friendship practice is the willingness, again, to expose one's own weakness and vulnerabilities, as we seek to understand, "who is my neighbor." Acts takes this idea a step further by stimulating the imagination of what one's story might look like if one were a part of a community that took Jesus' boundary breaking friendship activities seriously. Similarly, James links Jesus' friendship ethos to a practice that cultivates a community that assists the poor and stands up for social justice. Each of these deepen the responses to Jesus' own understanding of friendship in theologically transformative ways.

Finally, Jesus' friendship theology lives on not only in its New Testament expressions, but in the lived experiences of communities today. In this book, as I examined each of the New Testament expressions of Jesus' friendship, I have also related them to issues faced by contemporary communities. Jesus' own boundary breaking friendship activity holds implications that are as deeply profound and unsettling for the twenty-first century church as they were for the first century church. New Testament theologians cannot pretend to engage in scholarship that is somehow excluded from the needs of concerns of contemporary society. What I advocate, and what I have practiced throughout this book, is a correlational model of New Testament theology. Jesus' practice of engaging the misfits in his own society has implications for a church that is facing the challenge of reaching a society that is increasingly experiencing networked individualism. No longer can the church take for granted its ministry as service to people experiencing their life in highly localized communities. The networked individual is no longer bound to local communities and friendships as people were in the past. Nor can those whose lives are lived out through social media necessarily be thought of as losers and social isolates. When we look at Jesus' ministry to social outcasts, the implication for today is that the church must now occupy new social media spheres to reach out to individuals whose networks are almost entirely online and in the cloud. In my service as a New Testament professor, I occasionally am asked to preach at one or another of the many small rural congregations that are within a one hundred mile radius surrounding my university. Occasionally I post the sermons that I preach to the handful of folks gathered in these churches on my blog. I also post the link to my blog on my social media account. What is astounding to me now is the incredible reach such blog posts have. A sermon preached locally to a dozen souls can now reach dozens, sometimes even hundreds or more within a twenty-four hour period. While the jury may be out whether social media isolates us from local community, binds us to wider affinity networks, or both, those of us who are writing and teaching in this unique period of human history must take these dynamics into account.

The Synoptic Gospels and Reconciliation

Just as we must reckon with finding ways to communicate Jesus' boundary breaking theology into new cultural contexts, the New Testament writers also build upon Jesus' teachings on friendship with fresh expressions of their own. In Luke's parable of the Good Samaritan, we find the development of a biblical theology of reconciliation that can take us beyond our own echo chambers and comfort zones to engage with folks whose lives and communities we intersect daily, but with whom our interactions are spare and superficial, if not deeply discriminatory and conflict bound. Some of us may recognize in Jesus' conversation with the lawyer discussions we may have on occasion with trolls in our social media feeds. The lawyer is trying to trap Jesus, is using all kinds of techniques to justify himself, and he likely isn't interested in the central question that he asks, "and who is my neighbor?" Jesus, though, takes him on a "neighbor quest" through his parable. And through this "neighbor quest" we find an ethical perspective that can take us beyond superficial or even judgmental relationships with "outsiders." Too often, we have missed the import of the story by viewing it as a moralistic guide, that somehow, when Jesus tells the lawyer to "go and do likewise," he is to become like the Good Samaritan who crossed boundaries and helped the Jewish stranger and enemy. In my reading, since the lawyer is on his neighbor quest, the injunction to "go and do likewise" applies to his own brokenness and neediness. The lawyer won't experience friendship until he experiences himself the brokenness and vulnerability of the man who is beaten, robbed, and left to die on the side of the road. To "go and do likewise" means to make oneself entirely vulnerable, so that one can be helped and embraced by the other.

A biblical theology of embrace, as described by this reading of the Good Samaritan, entails a "double vision." Our need to see just reconciliation must be accompanied with our need to see the very real and human needs of the ones we are called to embrace. In the case of the lawyer engaging Jesus in Luke, as well as those social media trolls we might need, it likely means realizing one's own vulnerabilities as one is met with the embrace by the other. Mission Mississippi provides us a wonderful example of this double vision in action. Reconciliation between the races in the work of Mission Mississippi came about through simple and individual friendships that grew between members of black and white church participants. As these folks sat down to pray together, the white folks realized that—in prayer—they were becoming as vulnerable and broken as the man left to die on the side of the road. Similarly, it was a profound experience for the black members of Mission Mississippi to have the power to pray for the brokenness and needs of the ones who had wronged them, while also becoming vulnerable to former enemies through prayer. Each side not only looked to the need for a just reconciliation, but also to connect with each other on a very human level. Such embraces in prayer lay at the heart of the friendships created by Mission Mississippi. One can easily imagine how the practice of similar kinds of friendships might lead to a deep and life-giving theological reconciliation, a healing balm, a refreshing change in a time of culture war, and deep enmity among races, classes, and political parties.

John and Traumatized Community

In the beginning of the twenty-first century, tribalism and its aftermath dominates our national and global discourses in ways that the geopolitical ambitions of nation states dominated the discourse of the twentieth. Inherent in the Fourth Gospel is an all-encompassing ethical dualism between those who are children of the light and the surrounding darker world. Historically, therefore, the Fourth Gospel is a product of an emergent Christian community that was discovering its own identity by distinguishing itself from the norms and values of "the world." There are a number of outside groups who comprise "the world." Among the groups supposedly arrayed against the Johannine community are those Jewish authorities who rejected Jesus' messianic identity, gentiles and outsiders who did not share the religious values of the community, and others who excluded members of the community from their common rituals, and perhaps even persecuted it. To solidify its own group identity, the Fourth Gospel procures friendship language from the Greco-Roman world that originally applied to the experience of soldiers who had fought together and survived battle against a common enemy. Laying down one's life for another is a clear demonstration of one's commitment to the values and strivings of one's own tribe over against those aligned against it.

At first glance, using friendship language to establish or reinforce group identity vis-a-vis the outside world runs contrary to the ideas of embrace and reconciliation that I discussed as a friendship theology through my reading of the Good Samaritan passage. Likewise, enforcing the norms and values of an "in-group" also seems to run contrary to the historical Jesus' use of friendship to embrace the isolates and other outsiders. Indeed, in embracing the theology of the Fourth Gospel, one runs the risk of embracing a dualistic exclusivity that distinguishes between "us" and "them." It is a haunting and chilling experience to view the *Judensau* on the *Stadtkirche* in Wittenberg, the church where Luther preached. On it is a depiction in which Jews are suckling from the teats of a large sow, while a Rabbi lifts up the tail, all under the inscription, "Rabbini Schemhamphoris." It is important to know that the twentieth century Holocaust has its roots in an antisemitism that goes back to the Middle Ages. This foreground clearly demarcates the danger of texts like the Fourth Gospel, in which "the Jews" are depicted at times in such a negative light. Deriving a theology of friendship from such a dualistic work is an undertaking fraught with difficulty.

Nevertheless, when read from the perspective of contemporary veterans and others who may experience PTSD, John's friendship language has a deeper theological resonance. "I have said this to you, so that in me you may have peace . . . for I have conquered the world" (16:33) is the message of the Johannine Jesus. For the veteran who may still struggle with PTSD, Jesus' proclamation means that the combat is over; it has ended with a definitive victory. This is the irony of Jesus' death in John's Gospel. The cross is not a symbol of defeat, but of glory. When Jesus fashions a community of friends at the end of his Gospel, he is indeed creating a group of insiders, of people who understand and know his will in ways that outside forces may be unable to grasp. But like the veterans who have returned from war, for this community of insiders, the external conflict has ended. When Jesus lays down his life for his friends, he is not dying in defeat, but in victory. Jesus' sacrificial death in the Fourth Gospel not only creates community, it brings peace and expresses a final victory over the dark powers and principalities arrayed against it.

The message of the Fourth Gospel is not that the Johannine community will abide in fear or continuous conflict, but that they will abide in peace, precisely because Jesus has overcome the opposition. Ironically, those who have experienced the deep bonds of friendship in combat, those who continue to wrestle with the ongoing trauma and aftereffects of combat, may understand the deeper dimensions of this peace in ways that those who have not experienced such conflict cannot. While many readers may view the Fourth Gospel as a call to continuing dualistic conflict, veterans with PTSD are uniquely equipped to grasp the irony of Jesus' sacrificial death. The Johannine presentation of friendship is a word of hope. Contrary to cultural expectations of many characters within the Johannine narrative world, Jesus does not fall a casualty for his friends as part of an *ongoing* dualistic conflict. Quite the contrary, his death can be interpreted as a final victory that ends all such conflict. As such, veterans can teach us that the Fourth Gospel presents its readers a realized eschatology. It presents a hope that we can live in the now. Friendship is ours. Victory is now. Death is not a defeat. Peace, not conflict, is God's will for us and our community.

Acts and Imagination

The Gospels of Luke and John take Jesus' boundary breaking friendship theology and translate it into theological conceptions of reconciliation, peace, and community that offer deeply relevant hope to those of us who live in twenty-first century societies where racial division and post-traumatic stress are part of the everyday experience. But what is our conception of God that emerges from the friendship language of the New Testament community? In my chapter on Acts, I presented a theological framework that is dominating much of contemporary North American society's expression of God, Moralistic Therapeutic Deism (MTD). MTD presents a God who functions as a kind of divine butler and on-call therapist, a God whose only demand upon our lives is to be vaguely nice to one another. Writing in a period in which a kind of Moralistic Therapeutic Syncretism was part and parcel of Greco-Roman philosophical and ethical school, Luke presents in Acts a narrative in which God is richly engaged in the lives of other characters and in the formation of human community.

Not only are human beings social animals, as Aristotle claims, they also are storytelling animals. We derive meaning, joy, and a sense of purpose from experiencing rich and complex narratives. With the constant barrage of social media, consumerism, and hyper-capitalistic demands of work and stress upon our time, humans are becoming increasingly narratively deprived. Binge watching Netflix and other streaming services is part and parcel of that thirst. One Netflix study found that 61 percent of its users engage in binge watching, defined as watching between two to six episodes of the same TV show in one sitting, with 38 percent of them doing it alone.[3] In fact, Netflix has developed a "binge scale"

3. "Netflix Declares Binge Watching is the New Normal," Netflix Media Center, December 13, 2013. https://media.netflix.com/en/press-releases/netflix-declares-binge-watching-is-the-new-normal-migration-1.

in which genres are arrayed from those complex narratives that are watched slowly over time, political dramas like *House of Cards*, or historical dramas like *Peaky Blinders*, to simpler sci-fi, horror, and thriller narratives that are consumed quickly, like *Walking Dead* or *The Fall*. The idea is that such narratives are to be consumed serially, whether slowly or quickly, to satiate the human desire for story. I have often witnessed prolonged workplace conversations that center around these often superficial and ephemeral narratives.

Acts presents a narrative full of rich plot turns and complex characters. The church in Jerusalem grows at first at an astonishing rate, with a sense of community, shared possessions, hospitality, and joy that expands well beyond what many of us have experienced, even in our best communities. Yet, by chapter 8 this community is no longer the center of the narrative, and Saul's persecution scatters the believers in Judea. Acts presents us with Paul, a complex and not entirely reliable character, who starts off as a persecutor of the church, but ends up in custody in Rome, never quite able to fulfill his ambitious global mission, or indeed, to redeem his character. At every turn in this narrative the church experiences setbacks, miracles, and surprises. At every turn, God is present, one way or another, engaging in surprising and creative ways. The narrative summaries in Acts 2:41–47 and 4:32–35 present a God who is profoundly present in the friendships of those who heed Peter's call to repentance (2:38, 41). Borrowing language from the Greco-Roman friendship idiom, Luke tells us that the "believers share all things in common." Important to note is the shift in language here. Rather than saying, "friends have all things in common," as would have been expected in the Greco-Roman saying, Luke changes the key word from "friend" to "believer." While the Synoptic Gospels report Jesus as the one who is practicing and teaching a radical friendship to the marginalized, Acts presents God as the one responsible for binding human community. In much of the Greco-Roman thought on friendship, friendship involved the relationship between two individuals, usually males, usually high status elites. The move in Acts is one that takes us from such horizontal dipolar friendships between individuals to multipolar relationships in a newfound *koinonia* with God at the center in the vertical axis. Such friendships provide the basis for acts of hospitality, sharing possessions, and even engaging in bold speech to opponents of the community.

When reading texts like the Gospels and Acts, and arguably even Paul's letters, biblical theology properly engages the narrative imaginations of readers. Narratively deprived and addicted to a self-centered conception of God as a divine butler and on-call therapist, twenty-first century readers of the New Testament are not just primed but starving for its authentic narratives and depictions of a God who is surprising, creative, and community-authoring. Acts concludes with Paul in custody in Rome. The conclusion of Acts leaves the narrative open. God does not stop engaging the stories of the lives of individuals and communities with the end of apostolic period. The surprising, counterintuitive God that meets us in Acts is ready to author our communities, invite us to new friendships, share hospitality with people we thought we couldn't trust, share possessions with those who couldn't be more different from us, and speak prophetic justice to those with power and privilege.

Paul and Essential Brokenness

Paul makes extensive use of Greco-Roman friendship language in Philippians to describe God in Christ who fashions community through self-sacrificial activity. In the lead up to the Christ hymn in chapter 2, Paul describes a friendship that is enacted through self-humility and high regard for others. He calls on members of his community to prioritize the others' needs and well-being above one's own. By doing so, members of the Pauline community will have the same mind as Christ Jesus, who "empties himself" and "takes on the form of the slave" (2:5, 7). Paul's theological understanding of community is based in his Christology. Christ's self-abnegation becomes the model for Christian friendship and for the formation of Christian community. Christ, who was equal to God and indeed in the form of God (2:6), does not exploit this high status for his own purposes, but rather takes on the form of the human being, indeed the form of the slave. This reversal of power is core to understanding Pauline Christology. It is also essential for understanding Paul's understanding and admonitions to community.

The discourse of power provides us the key to understanding Paul's relevance for the lives of today's Christians. Jean Vanier has a certain conception of contemporary society in which he sees many people pulled into an experience of power that is ultimately detrimental to human flourishing. In contemporary Western society, self-authorship is a value that is prized above all others. The rugged self-made, self-reliant individual is still the ideal, especially for those who live in the hyper-consumeristic and hyper-capitalistic North American context. Life in such a society pits one individual against the other in an ever-escalating competition for more goods, services, and recognition. Life, work, even sport and leisure activities, are all part of a race to outperform the other, whether that means having a larger salary, a better title, or a newer, bigger house in a trendier neighborhood. Vanier, however, throughout his writings questions whether that conception of the human being accords with theological understanding. Here he places the discourse of disability to the forefront. He cautions those of us who are competing for power in life's rat race to step back and view life through the eyes of the disabled. The ones who are least able to succeed in contemporary society may be able to remind us what it means to be truly human again.

By talking about Christ taking on the form of the human being, even the slave, Paul's Christology is investing in the language of reverse *kalokagathia*. Greco-Roman culture associated virtue and human goodness with the beauty of the Greek male form. As my analysis in the above chapter indicates, by the time we get to the Roman period in which Paul is writing, the wealthier and higher status Roman households included slaves with various sorts of human deformities. Such slaves were kept as curiosities and as sport for high status Romans. Supposedly, by keeping such slaves around them, high status owners could be reminded of their own physical, mental, and ethical superiority. In contrast, Paul says that Christ took on the form of the human being, even the slave, and because of that God exalted him to Kurios, to Lord above all and before whom all human powers should kneel (2:9–11). In a grand reversal, the cross upon which Jesus dies, the place in which Christ's obedience and humility are on full display, ceases to represent a locus of shame, but becomes the place for Christ's exaltation.

The cross is the place where Vanier's theology and Paul's Christology meet. The same God who exalts Christ also "is at work" in us, "enabling" us to will and work for God's good pleasure (Phil 2:13). In Vanier's community, as in Paul's exhortation, human friendship is a cruciform expression, a reminder that through those places in which we are most broken, we experience the divine in each other. The long term members in Vanier's L'Arche communities, those who are mentally and physically disabled, provide experiences of transformative cruciformity. They rewire those who previously had been caught up in the rat race. They show that authentic Christian community is not about seeking one's own advantage, but about placing the needs and brokenness of the other as a priority above one's own. Deep and authentic friendship are not experienced in human striving for perfection, wealth, or power. Thriving human community is experienced in the common recognition of vulnerability and brokenness. For Vanier, and for Paul, cruciformity— loneliness, hurt, and rejection—are the common denominators for human experience. When we recognize our own brokenness and vulnerability to each other, we are primed to experience God's work in us, just as Christ experienced God's exaltation through obedience on the cross. What both Paul and Vanier recognize is that these kinds of friendships, friendships based upon human brokenness and need, are grounded in a narrative Christology in which God exalts the risen Christ who himself took on the form of a slave. For biblical theology, reading Philippians through the eyes of disability studies allows us to recognize that the Christian engagement of friendship language reverses societal expectations of what is good and beautiful. Authentic and thriving Christian community is grounded in cruciform humility and love.

James and a Renewed Ecclesia

When I began working on my dissertation on the friendship language in Acts at Princeton Theological Seminary, it was during a period of my life in which I was experiencing deep personal loneliness. There have been times in my life in which I was powerfully bound in community. I recall my years in Germany in which I had built up a strong network of friends who supported me and looked out for me. I remember my brief summer during seminary spent in a village in the highlands of Nicaragua. I also remember returning to the individualistic context of North America and feeling bewildered, abandoned, and broken, and yes, just so alone. The loneliness that so many Christians feel in the hyper-capitalistic societies in the North American and European contexts is a direct byproduct of a deluded and false understanding of ecclesiology. The number envy and competition among evangelical megachurches mirrors the consumeristic competition to build larger and larger malls. People flock to these large consumer edifices, sit in stadium seating (not pews), with the lights turned dim so they cannot even see their neighbor, much less the person sitting on the other side of the theater, and are entertained by professional musicians, lighting and stage show, and pastors who provide a feel-good message directly aimed toward individual and personal success. It is an alienating, bewildering, and lonely experience. Intimacy, true intimacy with God, with one's brother or sister in Christ, and especially with the poor and needy, is tossed aside in favor of ever greater numbers, larger buildings, and increasingly audacious ministries and mission trips that are aimed at providing congregations new and novel experiences. The contemporary church in North America is in crisis. This necessitates thinking biblically and theologically about what an authentic ecclesiology might look like.

James provides the basis for a wisdom ecclesiology that stands as a corrective to the excesses of the consumer church model. James's theology aligns God's cosmic will with human understanding. For James, the logos represents the will or plan of God that justice and righteousness prevail in the world. This logos

is implanted within each human being. The ones who align their will with God's universal justice can be considered God's friends, as they also are rejecting friendship with a world in which injustice, greed, and exploitation are present. This then is the basis for ecclesiology. The church is a collection of God's friends, those who embrace the will of God in their lives and in the world for justice and righteousness.

James's three themes of wisdom, social justice, and an activist faith are mirrored in the new monastic movement of the North American church. If there is to be a new model of church in the twenty-first century that rejects consumerism, shows deep solidarity with the poor, and demonstrates new dimensions of activist faith, it may well grow out of communities such as these. What is more, these communities are becoming laboratories for new and renewed understandings of friendship. Whether for a few months, or a period of years, those who join and live in these communities are learning again what it means to be God's church on earth. With their focus on racial and social justice, their community activism, and practices of communal prayer and worship, these communities provide a structure for authentic encounter with others. They are becoming centers for racial reconciliation and renewal. They are providing an alternative view of meaning that values individual difference, eschews a reliance upon stuff and consumerism for identity, and creates communal spaces for encountering the divine and exploring devotional purpose. Of course, not everyone is suited for life in this kind of community. For those who are suited, these new monastic communities provide anchors of meaningful community and beacons of authentic friendship in a sea of excess and consumerism. Theologians may well find such communities worthy resources to begin fresh discussions of what the church should look like in our contemporary world.

Conclusion

Throughout this book, I hope you as a reader have been stimulated to rethink how you are being called to reframe, rethink, and redefine friendship. The biblical text offers its readers worlds and friends, both old and new. By reading Scripture, if only for a moment, we set loose our imagination to enter narrative worlds where God is engaging the characters of the text in ways that are liberating, life-giving, and empowering. Through the text, God is also reaching out to us with offers of friendship. As we read, we experience God's friendship in various ways, perhaps as friendship with other readers, perhaps as friendship with the characters within the texts' stories, perhaps even as friendship with the biblical authors themselves. The biblical God enters our world to challenge assumptions, resurrect us from the dead, create community, and offer an invitation to embrace renewed creation. Ultimately, through Scripture, God is reaching out to offer us friendship, a friendship that will ground us with an ultimate sense of identity, purpose, and vocation in a deeply lonely, troubled, and broken world.

Bibliography

Aelred of Rievaulx. *Spiritual Friendship*. Translated by Lawrence C. Braceland. Collegeville, MN: Liturgical, 2010.

Aristotle. *Nicomachean Ethics*. Translated by Roger Crisp. Cambridge: Cambridge University Press, 2000.

Avalos, Hector, Sarah J. Melcher, and Jeremy Schipper. *This Abled Body: Rethinking Disabilities in Biblical Studies*. Leiden: Brill, 2007.

Bal, Mieke. *Narratology: Introduction to the Theory of Narrative*. 2nd ed. Toronto: University of Toronto Press, 1997.

Bhagat, Smiriti, et al. "Three and a Half Degrees of Separation." Facebook Research, February 4, 2016. https://research.fb.com/three-and-a-half-degrees-of-separation/.

Blount, Brian K. *Cultural Interpretation: Reorienting New Testament Criticism*. Minneapolis: Fortress, 1995.

———. *Then the Whisper Put on Flesh: New Testament Ethics in an African American Context*. Nashville: Abingdon, 2001.

Bohnenblust, Gottfried. "Beiträge Zum Topos Peri Filias." Ph.D. diss., Bern, 1905.

Booth, Wayne C. *The Company We Keep: An Ethics of Fiction*. Berkeley: University of California Press, 1988.

Brooks, David. "Donald Trump's Sad, Lonely Life." *New York Times*, Opinion, October 11, 2016. https://www.nytimes.com/2016/10/11/opinion/donald-trumps-sad-lonely-life.html.

Brown, Robbie. "Anti-Obama Protest at Ole Miss Turns Unruly." *New York Times*, November 7, 2012. https://www.nytimes.com/2012/11/08/us/anti-obama-protest-at-university-of-mississippi-turns-unruly.html.

Bultmann, Rudolf. *Theology of the New Testament*. 2 vols. Eugene, OR: Wipf and Stock, 1997; Prentice Hall, 1951.

Chambers, Andy. *Exemplary Life: A Theology of Church Life in Acts*. Nashville: B&H Academic, 2012.

Cicero. *On Old Age and on Friendship*. Translated by Frank O. Copley. Ann Arbor: University of Michigan Press, 1967.

Claiborne, Shane. *The Irresistible Revolution: Living as an Ordinary Radical.* Nashville: Zondervan, 2016.

Condon, Stephanie. "After 148 Years, Mississippi Finally Ratifies 13th Amendment, Which Banned Slavery." *CBS News*, February 18, 2013. https://www.cbsnews.com/news/after-148-years-mississippi-finally-ratifies-13th-amendment-which-banned-slavery/.

Culpepper, Alan R. *Anatomy of the Fourth Gospel: A Study in Literary Design.* Philadelphia: Fortress, 1983.

Culy, Martin M. *Echoes of Friendship in the Gospel of John.* Sheffield: Sheffield Phoenix, 2010.

Dillon, John M., and Jackson P. Hershbell, eds. *Iamblichus: On the Pythagorean Way of Life; Text, Translation and Notes.* SBL Texts and Translations 29. Atlanta: Scholars, 1990.

Dougherty, Kevin D. "How Monochromatic Is Church Membership? Racial-Ethnic Diversity in Religious Community." *Sociology of Religion* 64 (2003) 65–85.

Douglas, Mary. *Leviticus as Literature.* New York: Oxford University Press, 1999.

———. *Natural Symbols: Explorations in Cosmology.* New York: Vintage, 1973.

———. *Purity and Danger: An Analysis of Concepts of Pollution and Taboo.* New York: Praeger, 1970.

Duggins, Larry. *Together: Community as a Means of Grace.* Eugene, OR: Cascade, 2017.

Dupont, Jacques. "Community of Goods in the Early Church." In *The Salvation of the Gentiles: Essays on the Acts of the Apostles*, translated by John R. Keating, 85–109. New York: Paulist, 1967.

Elliott, Susan M. "John 15:15—Not Slaves but Friends: Slavery and Friendship Imagery and the Clarification of the Disciples." *Proceedings: Easter Great Lakes and Midwest Biblical Societies* 13 (1993) 31–46.

Everitt, Anthony. *Cicero: The Life and Times of Rome's Greatest Politician.* New York: Random House, 2003.

Fernholz, Tim. "More People Around the World Have Cell Phones than Ever Had Land-Lines." *Quartz*, February 25, 2014. https://qz.com/179897/more-people-around-the-world-have-cell-phones-than-ever-had-land-lines/.

Fiorenza, Elisabeth Schüssler. "The Ethics of Interpretation: De-Centering Biblical Interpretation." *Journal of Biblical Literature* 107 (1988) 3–17.

Fischer, Claude S. *Still Connected: Family and Friends in America since 1970.* New York: Russell Sage Foundation, 2011.

Fitzgerald, John T. "Christian Friendship: John, Paul, and the Philippians." *Interpretation* 61 (2007) 284–96.

———. *Friendship, Flattery, and Frankness of Speech: Studies on Friendship in the New Testament World.* Supplements to Novum Testamentum 82. Leiden: Brill, 1996.

―――. *Passions and Moral Progress in Greco-Roman Thought*. London: Routledge, 2008.

―――. "Philippians in the Light of Some Ancient Discussions of Friendship." In *Friendship, Flattery, and Frankness of Speech: Studies of Friendship in the New Testament World*, edited by John T. Fitzgerald, 141–60. Leiden: Brill, 1996.

―――, ed. *Greco-Roman Perspectives on Friendship*. Atlanta: Scholars Press, 1997.

Fredrickson, David E. "Παρρησια in the Pauline Epistles." In *Friendship, Flattery, and Frankness of Speech: Studies of Friendship in the New Testament World*, edited by John T. Fitzgerald. 163–83. Leiden: Brill, 1996.

Funk, Cary, and Greg Smith. "'Nones' on the Rise: One-in-Five Adults Have No Religious Affiliation." Pew Research Center, October 9, 2012. http://www.pewresearch.org/wp-content/uploads/sites/7/2012/10/NonesOnTheRise-full.pdf.

Furnish, Victor Paul. *The Love Command in the New Testament*. Nashville: Abingdon, 1972.

Garland, Robert. *The Eye of the Beholder: Deformity and Disability in the Graeco-Roman World*. Ithaca: Cornell University Press, 1995.

Gaventa, Beverly Roberts. *The Acts of the Apostles*. Nashville: Abingdon, 2003.

―――. "Toward a Theology of Acts: Reading and Rereading." *Interpretation* 42 (1988) 146–57.

Gradus, Jaimie L. "Epidemiology of PTSD." *PTSD: National Center for PTSD, U.S. Department of Veterans Affairs*. https://www.ptsd.va.gov/professional/treat/essentials/epidemiology.asp.

Grayling, A. C. *Friendship*. New Haven: Yale University Press, 2013.

Green, Joel. *The Gospel of Luke*. Grand Rapids: Eerdmans, 1997.

Hauerwas, Stanley. *The Peaceable Kingdom: A Primer in Christian Ethics*. Notre Dame: University of Notre Dame Press, 1983.

Heath, Elaine A., and Larry Duggins. *Missional, Monastic, Mainline: A Guide to Starting Missional Micro-Communities in Historically Mainline Traditions*. Eugene, OR: Cascade, 2014.

Heath, Elaine A., and Scott Thomas Kisker. *Longing for Spring: A New Vision for Wesleyan Community*. Eugene, OR: Cascade, 2010.

Horsley, Richard A. "Jesus and Empire." *Union Seminary Quarterly Review* 59 (2005) 44–74.

Hume, Douglas A. *The Early Christian Community: A Narrative Analysis of Acts 2:41–47 and 4:32–35*. Tübingen: Mohr Siebeck, 2011.

Inselmann, Anke. *Die Freude Im Lukasevangelium: Ein Beitrag Zur Psychologischen Exegese*. Tübingen: Mohr Siebeck, 2012.

Johnson, Luke Timothy. *The Acts of the Apostles*. Sacra Pagina 5. Collegeville, MM: Liturgical, 1992.

―――. *Brother of Jesus, Friend of God: Studies in the Letter of James*. Grand Rapids: Eerdmans, 2004.

————. "Making Connections: The Material Expression of Friendship in the New Testament." *Interpretation* 58 (2004) 158–71.

Juel, Donald. *Messianic Exegesis: Christological Interpretation of the Old Testament in Early Christianity.* Philadelphia: Fortress, 1988.

Junior, Nyasha, and Jeremy Schipper. "Disability Studies and the Bible." In *New Meanings for Ancient Texts: Recent Approaches to Biblical Criticisms and Their Applications,* edited by Steven L. McKenzie and John Kaltner, 21–37. Louisville, KY: Westminster John Knox, 2013.

Kelley, Nicole. "Deformity and Disability in Greece and Rome." In *This Abled Body: Rethinking Disabilities in Biblical Studies,* edited by Hector Avalos, Sarah J. Melcher, and Jeremy Schipper, 31–45. Leiden: Brill, 2007.

MacIntyre, Alasdair C. *After Virtue: A Study in Moral Theory.* 2nd ed. Notre Dame: University of Notre Dame Press, 1984.

Malherbe, Abraham J. "Paul's Self-Sufficiency (Philippians 4:11)." In *Friendship, Flattery, and Frankness of Speech: Studies of Friendship in the New Testament World,* edited by John T. Fitzgerald, 125–39. Leiden: Brill, 1996.

McPherson, Miller, Lynn Smith-Lovin, and Matthew E. Brashears. "Social Isolation in America: Changes in Core Discussion Networks Over Two Decades." *American Sociological Review* 71 (2006) 353–75.

Mitchell, Alan C. "'Greet the Friends by Name': New Testament Evidence for the Greco-Roman *Topos* on Friendship." In *Greco-Roman Perspectives on Friendship,* edited by John T. Fitzgerald. 225–62. Atlanta: Scholars Press, 1997.

————. "The Social Function of Friendship in Acts 2:44–47 and 4:32–37." *Journal of Biblical Literature* 111 (1992) 255–72.

Moltmann, Jurgen. *The Spirit of Life: A Universal Affirmation* Minneapolis: Fortress, 1992.

Newsom, Carol A. *The Book of Job: A Contest of Moral Imaginations.* Oxford: Oxford University Press, 2003.

Newton, Adam Zachary. *Narrative Ethics.* Cambridge: Harvard University Press, 1995.

Nussbaum, Martha Craven. "'Finely Aware and Richly Responsible': Literature and the Moral Imagination." In *Love's Knowledge: Essays on Philosophy and Literature,* 148–67. New York: Oxford University Press, 1990.

————. *The Fragility of Goodness: Luck and Ethics in Greek Tragedy and Philosophy.* Rev. ed. New York: Cambridge University Press, 2001.

————. "Introduction: Form and Content, Philosophy and Literature." In *Love's Knowledge: Essays on Philosophy and Literature,* 3–53. New York: Oxford University Press, 1990.

————. *The Therapy of Desire: Theory and Practice in Hellenistic Ethics.* Princeton: Princeton University Press, 1994.

O'Day, Gail R. "Jesus as Friend in the Gospel of John." *Interpretation* 58 (2004) 144–57.

Peterson, Brian K. "Philippians 2:5–11." *Interpretation* 58 (2004) 178–80.

Plutarch. *Moralia*. Translated by Frank Cole Babbitt. Cambridge: Harvard University Press, 1911.

Puthenkandathil, Eldho. *Philos: A Designation for the Jesus-Disciple Relationship: An Exegetico-Theological Investigation of the Term in the Fourth Gospel*. New York: Peter Lang, 1993.

Putnam, Robert D. *Bowling Alone: The Collapse and Revival of American Community*. New York: Simon & Schuster, 2000.

Rainie, Harrison, and Barry Wellman. *Networked: The New Social Operating System*. Cambridge: MIT Press, 2012. Kindle.

Resseguie, James L. *Narrative Criticism of the New Testament: An Introduction*. Grand Rapids: Baker Academic, 2005.

Reumann, John. "Philipians, Especially Chapter 4, as a 'Letter of Friendship': Observations on a Checkered History of Scholarship." In *Friendship, Flattery, and Frankness of Speech: Studies on Friendship in the New Testament World*, edited by John T. Fitzgerald, 83–106. Leiden: Brill, 1996.

Ringe, Sharon H. *Jesus, Liberation, and the Biblical Jubilee: Images for Ethics and Christology*. Philadelphia: Fortress, 1985.

———. *Wisdom's Friends: Community and Christology in the Fourth Gospel*. Louisville, KY: Westminster/John Knox Press, 1999.

Rose, Martha L. *The Staff of Oedipus: Transforming Disability in Ancient Greece*. Ann Arbor: University of Michigan Press, 2003.

Schaff, Philip, ed. *A Select Library of the Nicene and Post-Nicene Fathers of the Christian Church*. 14 vols. Grand Rapids: Eerdmans, 1956.

Schweitzer, Albert. *The Quest of the Historical Jesus*. Minneapolis: Fortress, 2001.

Slade, Peter. *Open Friendship in a Closed Society: Mission Mississippi and a Theology of Friendship*. New York: Oxford University Press, 2009.

Smith, Christian, and Melinda Lundquist Denton. *Soul Searching: The Religious and Spiritual Lives of American Teenagers*. New York: Oxford University Press, 2005.

Stassen, Glen. *Just Peacemaking: Transforming Initiatives for Justice and Peace*. Louisville, KY: Westminster/John Knox, 1992.

Tannehill, Robert C. *The Narrative Unity of Luke-Acts: A Literary Interpretation*. 2 vols. Philadelphia: Fortress, 1986–1991.

Taylor, T. Andrew, and Michael E. Sherr. "When Veterans Come Home." *Family and Community Ministries* 21 (2008) 6–16.

Vanier, Jean. *Becoming Human*. New York: Paulist, 1998.

———. *Befriending the Stranger*. London: Darton, Longman, and Todd, 2005.

———. *Made for Happiness: Discovering the Meaning of Life with Aristotle*. Translated by Kathryn Spink. Toronto: Anansi Press, 2001.

Wang, Hua, and Barry Wellman. "Social Connectivity in America: Changes in Adult Friendship Network Size from 2002 to 2007." *American Behavioral Scientist* 53 (2010) 1148–69.

Weems, Lovett H., Jr. "No Shows." *Christian Century* 127 (2010) 10–11.

Wendel, Ulrich. *Gemeinde in Kraft: Das Gemeindeverständnis in Den Summarien Der Apostelgeshichte.* Neukirchen: Neukirchner, 1998.

Wilson-Hartgrove, Jonathan. *New Monasticism: What It Has to Say to Today's Church.* Grand Rapids: Brazos 2008.

Witetschek, Stephan. "The Stigma of a Glutton and Drunkard: Q 7,34 in Historical and Sociological Perspective." *Ephemerides theologicae Lovanienses* 83 (2007) 135–54.

Wrenhaven, Kelly L. *Reconstructing the Slave: The Image of the Slave in Ancient Greece.* London: Bristol Classical Press, 2012.

Wu, Tim. *The Attention Merchants: The Epic Scramble to Get Inside Our Heads.* New York: Knopf, 2016.

Scripture Index

SCRIPTURE INDEX

Index

Made in the USA
Middletown, DE
31 January 2020